CHRISTIANITY AND MONEY

IS VOLUME

59

OF THE

Twentieth Century Encyclopedia of Catholicism

UNDER SECTION

V

THE LIFE OF FAITH

IT IS ALSO THE

17TH

VOLUME IN ORDER OF PUBLICATION

Edited by HENRI DANIEL-ROPS *of the* Académie Française

CHRISTIANITY AND MONEY

By *JACQUES LECLERCQ*

Translated from the French by ERIC EARNSHAW SMITH

HAWTHORN BOOKS · PUBLISHERS · New York

First Edition, May, 1959
Second Printing, November, 1960

NIHIL OBSTAT

Johannes M. T. Barton, S.T.D., L.S.S.

 Censor Deputatus

IMPRIMATUR

E. Morrogh Bernard

 Vicarius Generalis

Westmonasterii, die XVI JANUARII MCMLIX

CONTENTS

INTRODUCTION

This book deals with an aspect of Christianity which is in striking opposition to many characteristic tendencies of the modern world. It is true that the attitude of Christianity towards the subject of our discussion has always been opposed to that of the world; but its opposition to the modern world has changed in conformity with the revolutionary changes brought about in economic life by the advent of technical civilization. No doubt there are other tendencies of the modern world more receptive to the Christian idea. Nevertheless, the tendencies with which we are concerned are not only fundamental but occupy the foremost place in public affairs.

At the same time, the aspect of Christian teaching which concerns us here is itself fundamental, covering as it does to a certain extent the whole of life both public and private, collective and individual. The Christian attitude to money reveals itself in the monastic vow of poverty no less than in the social teaching of the encyclicals. It concerns itself with the board of directors of a company no less than with the housewife's purchases at the greengrocer's. Christianity cannot be understood without an understanding of Christ's attitude towards worldly goods.

Yet the Christian attitude with regard to earthly values is equally incomprehensible unless considered in the context of the Christian synthesis. There is nothing arbitrary, fantastic or irrational about the Christian attitude to money, which is firmly rooted in revelation. It is inseparable from the whole corpus of Christian teaching; and though this volume deals with the particular question of the Christian attitude to money, our discussion necessarily involves a reference to at least some of the presuppositions or basic truths of Christian teaching.

Our title is "Christianity and Money", because it is in terms of money that the problem is most frequently presented: Christ himself in the Gospels habitually speaks of riches, of the renunciation of riches, and of poverty in the sense of lack of money.

It must not, however, be forgotten that this conception of poverty applies to all worldly goods. It applies to intelligence, and in the modern world to the certificates which are presumed to guarantee the possession of intelligence. An intelligent man is as proud of his intelligence as a millionaire of his millions; or to put it more accurately, intelligence is a form of wealth. Nowadays not to hold a certificate can often brand one as an ignoramus.

The possession of physical beauty, strength and style is as much a source of pride as the possession of literary or artistic talent. The pride and vanity of writers, artists, public speakers and actors is a matter of common knowledge. Generally speaking, the possessor of any inherited or acquired talent runs the risk of succumbing to egotism and pride.

The Scriptures and the sages reiterate the question "What have you that you have not received?" But the question meets with no response, for men regard their possessions not as something entrusted to them to be used in the service of the Lord, but as something belonging to themselves to be used for their own purposes. These selfish purposes consist either in the enjoyment of possessions, or in using them for self-assertion or self-aggrandizement, or as a means to acquiring a fortune, which brings us back to money, the customary common denominator.

One sometimes comes across scientists who are wholly immersed in the work of their laboratory and apparently untouched by any human ambition. But scratch the surface, and one finds them eaten up with the proud consciousness of their superiority to the despised man in the street, and on the whole so absorbed in themselves and their work as to seem forgetful of their dependence on a Creator. These are exceptional cases: their heads are in the clouds but they are no less self-centred and enslaved by their own pursuits than the rest of mankind.

The average man envisages worldly goods in terms of money, which is the means to obtain all other goods. Money is the theme both of the Gospel and of contemporary debate. Whether money actually *is* wealth, or merely its expression or a simple means to obtaining something else, we always come back to money. Consequently the title of our book remains valid, although we shall not confine ourselves to the discussion of money alone.

Money is a symbol. We shall frequently have occasion in the following pages to treat of other matters, and the reader must never forget that money, in spite of the importance universally attached to it, is worthless apart from its human context. It is everything and it is nothing. Behind it stand the whole of life and all human goods, from all of which it cannot properly be isolated.

On the other hand, worldly goods expose us to a twofold danger, absorption in material things and absorption in ourselves. We are tempted to centre everything on human happiness, forgetting that man's greatness, perfection and happiness, his whole meaning in fact, consist in transcending the commonly accepted human good. There is the further danger of allowing ourselves and our happiness to govern all our activities, of becoming self-centred and self-satisfied. Worldly goods make a man boastful and materialistic. The more a man devotes his life to material things, the more sub-human does he become, for it is the mind which differentiates him from the lower creatures. Self-satisfaction does not derogate from his human status, but it cuts him off from God, and if he fails fully to realize his human destiny by transcending the demands imposed by the human condition, his proud withdrawal into himself will prevent his self-realization.

The explanation of these facts will occupy us throughout the rest of this book.

CHAPTER I

BASIC TRUTHS

We shall begin by calling attention to some of the basic truths which form the starting point of Christ's teaching, from which all the rest follows automatically.

GOD IS A FATHER

This is perhaps the most important truth preached by Christ.

Christ is at the same time the witness to and the preacher of the fatherhood of God. Constantly he uses the words "My Father and your Father". In the parables God appears as the father of a family, an expression which includes the idea of providence as well as the profounder idea of love.

It is St John who lays the greatest emphasis on love. "God is love" (1 John 4. 8, 16), and "if we love one another, then we have God dwelling in us, and the love of God has reached its full growth in our lives" (*ibid*. 12). The whole of St John's first epistle is devoted to the identification of God with love.

God is so exalted that when men find him by their unaided efforts they at first experience a feeling of being crushed. They look on God as "the Other", as a being different at all points from themselves, an attitude expressed in Catholic theology by the term "the transcendence of

God". The wisdom of the East describes God as "the In-effable", he of whom nothing can be said. Even Greek philosophy failed to explain how God can be in relation with the world. He is the Perfect, the Omniscient, the Omnipotent. The Jews laid most stress on his power. But Christ said: He is the Father, my Father and your Father. He is love.

Love is an abstract idea: in the synoptic gospels God is above all the Father. "When thou givest alms, thou shalt not so much as let thy left hand know what thy right hand is doing, so secret is thy almsgiving to be; and then thy Father, who sees what is done in secret, will reward thee" (Matt. 6. 3–4). The same injunction applies to prayer (*ibid*. 6) and to fasting (*ibid*. 17–18): "thy Father, who sees what is done in secret, will reward thee."

It follows that our relations with God are *personal*, like those of a child with its father. The Father cares for us. "He takes every hair of your head into his reckoning" (Matt. 10. 30).

Fatherhood is identified with providence, but Christian providence is a loving providence. Love, fatherhood and providence are three overlapping ideas.

The general picture we carry away is of God as an active person, a "you", a father to be addressed and trusted and obeyed. "Do not fret then" over your needs; "you have a Father in heaven who knows that you need them all" (Matt. 6. 32).

The Christian attitude is therefore principally one of trust. Most people find this hard of acceptance. Most Christians continue to accept the pagan and Jewish idea of God as an all-powerful tyrant whose favour must be won by flattery, so that our prayers may be granted. They do not trust him. They do not look on him as the loving Father who wishes us well and knows better than ourselves

what is good for us. The majority of mankind cannot understand such an idea, in spite of the fact that Christ himself
constantly preached it. Men mistrust God, and approach
him warily. They cannot surrender themselves to him.

Nevertheless Christ also said: "Ask and the gift will
come; seek, and you shall find; knock and the door shall
be opened to you." The apparent contradiction is resolved
by trust. If our relation to God is like that of a child to
a wise and loving father, we shall give spontaneous expression to everything that comes into our mind; thoughts and
feelings as they occur will be revealed to him, in the cer-
tainty that our Father in heaven will "give wholesome gifts
to those who ask him" (Matt. 7. 11).

The door between heaven and earth lies open for us to
pass from one to the other. God is among us, he sees us
and watches over us. Life is an unending dialogue between
man and God. Nothing is hidden from him.

Isaias, addressing the Jews, had said: "My thoughts are
not your thoughts, said the Lord, and your ways are not
my ways" (Isaias 55. 8). Jesus teaches that our ways *ought*
to be God's ways, even though we do not understand them.
To do the will of my Father in heaven. . . . He is indeed
in heaven, but he is also on earth. God cannot be localized.
"The kingdom of heaven will not give entrance to every
man who calls me Master, Master; only to the man that
does the will of my Father who is in heaven" (Matt. 7. 21).
And the kingdom of heaven is not to be sought for in
some imaginary empyrean; it is "here, within you" (Luke
17. 21).

All this is so remote not only from our present-day
materialism, but from the old religions which placed the
abode of God in some inaccessible beyond, that Christianity
acquires a unique meaning. It was this fundamental truth
that Christ came down to preach, and this "good news" is

so far beyond the human range that few can understand it. The true Christian is above all he who accepts the teaching of the fatherhood of God and shapes his conduct accordingly.

CHRISTIANITY'S APPEAL TO THE INDIVIDUAL

Christ appeals to each one of us; he died for each individual one of us. "I thought of thee in mine agony, I have sweated such drops of blood for thee."[1] The Christian mystery is a mystery of personal union between the Christian and God and the Saviour.

Christ was not a social reformer. There were, it is true, social reformers both before and during his lifetime. Plato and Aristotle and the Gracchi were social reformers, but the call of Jesus was to *conversion*.

Conversion is a *personal* matter: it is the individual who is converted. The Christian problem is to turn towards God, to look upon him as a father and to live in accordance with his will. God is the concern of the individual: Conversion takes place in the depths of the conscience, when the individual surrenders himself freely to God.

This phenomenon is observable in all religions, but is lacking in what is now called "lay mysticism". For the last two centuries mankind has increasingly directed its attention to social affairs, that is to the problem of organizing communal life. The modern world is to a large extent dominated by social doctrines which aim at promoting human welfare by organization. Herein consists the social question: how is society to be so organized that justice and happiness may prevail? Hence the importance attributed to politics and economics, which are concerned with the organization of the State, of production and of trade.

[1] Pascal's *Pensées*, Everyman Edition, p. 149.

Christ said: "Blessed are the clean of heart; they shall see God" (Matt. 5. 8). Nothing similar is to be found in our discussions on parliamentary versus people's democracy, or on a free versus a communist economy.

Christ addresses himself to each individual soul, saying "Come and follow me". It is to each one of us that he speaks. Christianity presents a problem which every individual must solve for himself and by himself. The Christian is not a conscript: his attitude is adopted of his own free choice.

For this reason the social question is not mentioned in the Gospels. Questions of this kind were sometimes put to our Saviour, in the attempt to force him to take sides in some political or social controversy; but he always put them aside. It is to the soul that he addresses a personal appeal, it is the individual who must decide on his response. There is no intermediary between the Christian and his God.

Henceforth we can rest assured that the Christian problem cannot in itself be a social problem. The Christian lives in society, and he will be guided in the performance of his social duties by his faith, in the light of which he will do his best to assert the Christian values. But his true life as a Christian is a life in God, a life turned towards God, fed by God, and responsible to God's will. It is consequently the leaven to which our Lord likened the kingdom of heaven (Matt. 13. 33).

INCARNATION

But God is in our midst. He is in us, he unites himself to us, he takes us up into himself. All these things are what we mean by incarnation.

In the first place the Word became flesh and dwelt

among us, becoming one of us. Jesus was a man, at first sight like other men. It was only gradually that his companions came to recognize in him something superhuman.

Furthermore, to the disciples who followed him Jesus made the gift of his life. He saved them not only by offering to the Father a redemptive love which was the very love of God, nor by his own suffering and death on the cross. He went further, by sharing his disciples' life, penetrating it and transforming it by his presence within the soul. The disciple himself becomes Christ, because Christ lives in him not as a foreign body but as a source of life, so that we may interpret literally the words "I am alive; or rather, not I; it is Christ that lives in me" (Gal. 2. 20).

"I am the vine, you are its branches" (John 15. 5). There is a spark of the divine in us. To submit ourselves to Christ through faith means not only believing in him and following his example, but inviting him—together with the Father and the Holy Spirit—to take possession of our heart and to dwell in it, so that our personality, our heart, mind and behaviour become his, not only in the sense of following in his steps, but in the much more precise sense that it is Christ who acts and thinks in our actions and thoughts to the extent to which we allow our lives to be lived by him.

This is what theology means by the supernatural life. It is conferred on us by baptism, when for the first time we give ourselves to Christ, and is afterwards developed throughout our life as Christians. Thus through the Christian the life of Christ continues to be lived on earth, he is for ever at work in the world. His activity may be measured by the faithfulness of his disciples. The object of the Christian life is to allow Christ to continue living and working among us.

Incarnation takes place within our human nature. Just as Christ was a man subject to human limitations, so the

Christian remains fully man, and human life is transformed by the divine life, which endows it with spirit while leaving its natural conditions unchanged. God *in us*. By these emphatic words we mean that we remain men, that we retain our human nature, and that Christ has taken that nature upon him. The Gospel words "made flesh" are no mere figure of speech. When Christ rested by the well of Jacob he experienced real fatigue, and after fasting he experienced real hunger.

In the same way the Christian remains wholly man, but is at the same time filled by God. God expresses himself through man, but since it is God who is expressing himself everything is changed, although the human conditions of his self-expression subsist.

It follows that no morality is more permeated by the divine than Christian morality. God is in everything, God expresses himself in everything: the sole problem is to allow God to express himself through us. Yet at the same time no morality is more human, more docile to the physical, mental and social limitations imposed by the human condition. Christian morality preaches not withdrawal from the world, but a surrendering of the world to God. The fact that some Christians, followed by some non-Christians, have held the contrary view of the incompatibility between Christian morality and the assertion of human values, only goes to show that they have never understood the Christianity preached by Christ himself.

COMMUNITY

Human circumstances involve living in a community—a better, because more general term than society. Man lives in a community, and the community is the most important feature of human life.

On the supernatural plane, community, such as we encounter it at all times and in all places, takes the form of human fellowship in sin and redemption, of the community of saints, and of the Church. It is true that the Christian life is an individual life, a dialogue between man and God, and that my relation to God is strictly personal: nevertheless I should not be a Christian had not God made use of other men to pass on the faith to me. "How are they to believe in him, until they listen to him? And how can they listen, without a preacher to listen to?" (Romans 10. 14).

Accordingly, whether it is a question of family, profession or government, of civil, political or economic affairs, the Christian is bound by the conditions of human nature. The Church herself is the most striking demonstration of this truth.

Because Christ becomes flesh, his Church is necessarily a human society, composed of human beings and subject to human conditions, but at the same time dependent on the loyalty of her members to our Saviour. To the extent in which Christ's presence vivifies her, the Church carries on her work in the world; to that extent she conveys her message to the world, to that extent Christ is present in the world.

It is true that God has bestowed on the Church a guarantee of eternal life. Infallibility and apostolic succession vouch for her possession of the authentic tradition and of the life of Christ. Nevertheless these two guarantees, though fundamental, operate in the human field, and the Holy Spirit in the Church works so naturally under human conditions that history may be written as a record of merely natural events without any reference to divine intervention. It is of the essence of incarnation that everything takes place as if there were nothing beyond the world of nature; yet there is something beyond, and as if by chance something occurs within the framework of normal experience to upset all our calculations.

It follows that in a certain sense the whole Christian problem is the problem of the Church, in spite of the fact that in another sense it is the problem of the individual Christian's adherence to the Father through Christ. No contradiction is involved, because our personal adherence leads us to the Church, which is the instrument by which God works in the world in general and in my heart in particular. To be a Christian is to come to Christ, but it is in the Church that we find him.

CHRISTIANITY A SPIRITUAL RELIGION

Christianity, a religion based on the idea of incarnation, changes the whole of life, and yet in some way leaves it unchanged, since the Christian remains a human being. For this reason the world is always baffled no less by Christ than by the Church and the individual Christian. Christ is accused of being at one and the same time both ordinary and extraordinary. The Church is accused of compromising with the world and at the same time of not understanding human nature. The man in the street is uneasy when he meets a Christian, whose values he perceives to be different: he blames him for the same faults that he finds in Christ and in the Church. Human, too human, inhuman. He would feel more comfortable in the company of a cynic like Diogenes or a yogi who has totally renounced the world; he recognizes the gulf between them and himself, and knows where he is. But with a Christian one never knows where one is. The reason is that Christianity is a spiritual religion. The changes it effects take place not in the realm of matter but in the realm of spirit, the realm of the will. It induces a man to do the same things but to do them in a different spirit. The Christian works as hard and at the same tasks as his fellow men, but his aim differs from theirs. Like them, nevertheless, he will take the necessary steps for the successful realization of his purpose.

Christianity is a purely spiritual religion, that is a religion of moral values. "Moral" values are those which appeal only to the mind. For an animal there are no moral values. In mankind eating becomes a moral value in so far as the material act is associated with a value which we call spiritual because it is appreciated only by the mind. Feasting is man's way of celebrating a wedding or even a religious festival: no animal feasts.

Christianity, while allowing human life to pursue its normal course—for God is sparing of miracles—brings about a change of purpose, and establishes its own scale of values, which are not the values of the world. "My ways are not your ways": "Blessed are those who mourn". In accordance with its own scale of values it esteems what the world contemns, and contemns what the world esteems.

To understand the Christian scale of values we must look to Christ, listen to him, and discover what he thinks good for us and what he thinks harmful. Then only shall we understand how a Christian deals with the problem of money and of worldly goods in general.

CHAPTER II

CHRIST'S ATTITUDE TOWARDS RICH AND POOR

BLESSED ARE THE POOR

"Father, who art Lord of heaven and earth, I give thee praise that thou hast hidden all this from the wise and prudent, and revealed it to little children" (Matt. 11. 25). The Gospels are full of Christ's love for the children and the humble. On the human plane the child and the poor man are essentially one. "When thou givest hospitality, invite poor men to come, the cripples, the lame, the blind" (Luke 14. 13). Every kind of trouble is associated by Jesus with poverty: yet he speaks of giving hospitality, which is a prerogative of the rich. He does not insist on a rich man's becoming poor.

"When thou givest a dinner or a supper, do not ask thy neighbours to come, or thy brethren, or thy kindred, or thy friends who are rich" (Luke 14. 12). Jesus does not say that a man must not be rich, but he loves the poor. His meaning becomes clear when we consider the reason he gives for not inviting the rich: "It may be they will send thee invitations in return, and so thou wilt be recompensed for thy pains." Gifts to the poor are free like love, and expect no recompense.

"Blessed are you who are poor; the kingdom of God is yours" (Luke 6. 20). Matthew's words are "Blessed are the poor in spirit" (5. 3), and the variant warns us that Jesus is a preacher, not a pedant. The difference of wording is of no consequence. Jesus is a prophet. Whether "poor" or "poor in spirit", it is the spirit that matters. A man may be poor in the material sense but at the same time a money-grubber, in which case he forfeit's Christ's blessing.

Later commentators, pleading reverence for the words of God, have tried to keep close to the meaning of Christ's sayings by detaching them from their context and interpreting them "in themselves". We shall see how the true meaning is perverted by this piecemeal treatment. No saying should ever be dealt with out of its context.

"Listen to me, my dear brethren; has not God chosen the men who are poor in the world's eyes to be rich in faith, to be heirs of that kingdom which he has promised to those who love him?" (James 2. 5). It is the poor whom Jesus loves, because they are the little children, the humble, the unfortunate. In the beatitudes it is not only the poor who are called blessed, but also the patient, those who mourn and those who hunger, the merciful and the peace-makers. A blessing is given not only to the unfortunate, but also to those who practise the virtues of submission and kindliness. The beatitudes form a whole, from which the blessing on the poor must not be isolated.

A MAN CANNOT BE MY DISCIPLE UNLESS...

"None of you can be my disciple if he does not take leave of all that he possesses.... Great multitudes bore him company on his way; to these he turned, and said: If any

man comes to me, without hating his father and mother
and wife and children and brethren and sisters, yes, and his
own life too, he can be no disciple of mine. A man cannot
be my disciple unless he takes up his own cross, and follows
after me" (Luke 14. 33, 25–7).

This saying has parallels in the other synoptic Gospels.
Once again we notice how the renunciation of possessions
is treated as on an equal footing with all other kinds of
renunciation, such as renunciation of human affections and
acceptance of hardship. The Sermon on the Mount is a
kind of code of renunciation, beginning with the beatitudes
which may be summed up in the formula: Blessed are the
unfortunate in the eyes of the world.

Against these blessings Luke sets four maledictions,
addressed in the first place to the rich:

"Woe upon you who are rich; you have your comfort
already.

"Woe upon you who are filled full; you shall be hungry.

"Woe upon you who laugh now; you shall mourn and
weep.

"Woe upon you, when all men speak well of you; their
fathers treated the false prophets no worse" (Luke 6.
24–6).

There follow the precepts of love, forgiveness and renunciation which are also to be found in the Sermon on
the Mount.

It is one of the dominating ideas of the Gospels: what the
world calls happiness is no happiness for the Christian.
Christian happiness does not consist in worldly goods.

THE PARABLE OF THE RICH YOUNG MAN

We now come to the best known and most discussed of
the parables, which eventually assumed such importance

that a whole system of ethics was based on it. The story is told in all three Synoptics, with slight but significant variations. I shall first quote the whole passage from Mark, and then discuss the variants.

> Then he went out to continue his journey; and a man ran up and knelt down before him, asking him, Master, who art so good, what must I do to achieve eternal life? Jesus said to him, Why dost thou call me good? None is good, except God only. Thou knowest the commandments, Thou shalt not commit adultery, Thou shalt do no murder, Thou shalt not steal, Thou shalt not bear false witness, Thou shalt not wrong any man, Honour thy father and thy mother. Master, he answered, I have kept all these ever since I grew up. Then Jesus fastened his eyes on him, and conceived a love for him; In one thing, he said, thou art still wanting. Go home and sell all that belongs to thee; give it to the poor, and so the treasure thou hast shall be in heaven; then come back and follow me. At this, his face fell, and he went away sorrowing, for he had great possessions. And Jesus looked round, and said to his disciples, With what difficulty will those who have riches enter God's kingdom! The disciples were amazed at his words; but Jesus gave them a second answer, My children, how hard it is for those who trust in riches to enter God's kingdom! It is easier for a camel to pass through a needle's eye, than for a man to enter the kingdom of God when he is rich. They were still more astonished; Why then, they said to themselves, who can be saved? Jesus fastened his eyes on them, and said, Such things are impossible to man's powers, but not to God's; to God, all things are possible (Mark 10. 17–27).

Then follows the passage quoted above from Luke, promising the kingdom to all who have forsaken everything.

This is Mark's version. Matthew speaks of a "young man", and Luke of "a ruler" (*princeps*). It is Matthew who has given its classic name to the story of "the rich young man". Moreover, when the young man replies that he has always kept the commandments of the law, it is Matthew who reports Jesus as saying, "If thou hast a mind to be perfect, go home and sell all" etc., whereas in Mark and Luke Jesus simply says, "In one thing thou art still wanting. . . ."

This is the most important detail of all, for the text of Matthew provides the basis for the tradition according to which the renunciation of riches is not obligatory. Only the law is binding; renunciation of riches is merely *suggested* to whoever wishes to be perfect. And a tradition has grown up according to which the poverty mentioned in the Gospels and proposed by Jesus to the rich young man is a mere recommendation, which need not be carried out to achieve salvation. This theory has been put into practice in the rules of religious poverty.

The tradition, however, encounters serious difficulties.

It can be explicitly stated as follows. A Christian is by no means required to bestow his possessions on the poor, and can achieve salvation without so doing. The poverty recommended by Jesus is a counsel of perfection; but no man is obliged to be perfect, or even to strive after perfection.

At first sight, when one compares the three texts one is amazed that so important a doctrine should be based on a variant reading occurring in only one out of the three Gospels. For the doctrine is undoubtedly important; it plays a considerable part in the practice of Christian life. Yet the Gospel authors clearly attached little importance to the variant, otherwise they would have paid more attention to it; and in any case it would seem more reasonable to rely on the version given by two of them rather than on that given by one alone. Moreover, the words used by

Mark and Luke are exactly the same: "In one thing thou art still wanting."

On the other hand, the commandments first referred to by Jesus, which the young man or the ruler had always hitherto observed, are the commandments of the Jewish law. It is surely incredible that Christ's additional injunction is merely optional, a suggestion thrown out to any well-wisher who might be disposed to follow him, and that, in short, a disciple of Jesus need do no more than continue to obey the precepts of the Jewish law.

When we consider the meaning of the incarnation and redemption, and call to mind the tragedy of the cross, we must rather be astonished that our Saviour should have appeared on earth simply for the purpose of setting an optional idea before a few chosen disciples. It is true that poverty is not the sum total of the Christian law, but it occupies an important place in the teaching of the Gospels, and Christ's references to it are not confined to the story of the rich young man. If it is possible for a rich man to be a good Christian while retaining his possessions, what are we to make of the malediction "Woe upon you who are rich"?

In this same parable, moreover, when the rich young man has departed, Christ says: "With what difficulty will those who have riches enter God's kingdom!" But if they are under no compulsion to give up their riches, where is the difficulty? We appear to be confronted with a course of action which is binding on nobody, yet is essential for entering the kingdom.

A solution to our difficulty may perhaps once more be found by examining another variant in the Gospel accounts. According to Matthew and Luke, Jesus says that it will be difficult for those who have riches to enter God's kingdom; but according to Mark he says: "How hard it is for those *who trust* in riches. . . ." The delicate variation in Mark's account is the more striking in contrast with the habitual plainness of his style.

In any case the general situation is clear: Jesus asks the young man to give up his possessions, and the young man refuses; the reason can only be that he clings to them. All our previous quotations assert that a Christian should cling to nothing, but be ready to give up everything for the sake of the Kingdom. "He is not worthy of me, that loves father or mother more; he is not worthy of me, that loves son or daughter more" (Matt. 10. 37). What our Saviour asks of us, we should be proud to give him immediately.

In short, Christ's attitude of mind is very different from that which came later to prevail, even in moral theology. The theologian had to deal with average Christians, baptized at birth but unwilling to follow Christ, who are only concerned to save their souls at the least possible cost. He therefore tried to restrict his demands to what is reasonable. His views were coloured by his desire to be merciful; in this, as in many other respects, he tried to avoid overburdening the conscience. Very different was the attitude of Jesus.

The average Christian worships money. He wants as much as he can get, and would prefer to keep what he has and to part with as little as possible. Faced by a divine law which disturbs him with its different scale of values, he asks himself just how much he may keep without contravening the law, and how much he should give away in order to "square" his conscience. "Squaring" seems remote from the Gospel point of view. The life to which Christ calls us is a life of whole-hearted love, and whole-heartedness is incompatible with the constant calculation of the extent of our obligations. In practice our "average" Christian is calculating only when it is a question of giving: when it is a question of adding to his wealth he succumbs to every form of covetousness.

Christ's attitude is therefore clear. We are dealing not with a material situation but with an attitude of mind. Worldly goods, and riches in particular, make us worldly minded: our problem is to achieve detachment. But detachment is difficult. We live surrounded by our possessions. Never for one moment can we forget the enjoyment we derive from them, the attention they demand, the satisfaction they provide to our self-esteem in demonstrating our success to the world. Worldly goods are a tyrant: it seemed to Christ beyond the power of mortal man to escape their tyranny except by getting rid of them. "Where your treasure-house is, there your heart is too." For Christ the conclusion to be drawn is plain: "You must serve God or money; you cannot serve both" (Matt. 6. 21, 24).

It is accordingly a question of serving, not of possessing. Wealth is adventitious, the service of God is everything. If we do not make worldly goods our treasure we shall find it easy to renounce them. The rich young man could not bring himself to renounce his riches: on hearing Christ's words he at once "went away sorrowing". His treasure was not in heaven; he could spare only a part of it for God. But to Jesus a share is not acceptable. Renunciation of possessions is only a symbol: the essential is complete self-surrender.

JESUS AND THE RICH

We have already remarked that Jesus was not an academic teacher. His teaching is not confined to abstract propositions, but reveals itself in his attitude of mind. We have noted his attitude towards poverty and wealth; but he also encountered a number of individual rich men, from whose behaviour as depicted in the parables a lesson may also be drawn.

In the Gospels we meet rich men who are also good men, whose wealth is not made a subject of reproach.

At the very outset we meet the wise men, persons of rank and birth, who brought their costly gifts as an offering to the infant Jesus. No criticism is brought against them, any more than against the aged Simeon. It is as persons of importance and understanding that they are represented in the Gospel.

Among other rich men we might mention Zacchaeus, Joseph of Arimathea, and perhaps Lazarus who was raised from the dead. Indeed, in everyday life Jesus seems to take little interest in the question of riches. He consorts equally with rich and poor, and his feelings in each case are governed by the character of the individual.

The most characteristic story is that of Zacchaeus (Luke 19. 1–10). Zacchaeus was a rich tax-farmer. These publicans, as they were called by the Romans, formed a social class which no longer exists today, but whose standing was roughly that of a modern stockbroker. Theirs was a profession in which it was easy to become rich, but difficult to remain entirely honest. Their practice was to take the proceeds of a tax on payment of a fixed sum, and to reimburse themselves by extracting what they could from the tax-payer, their profit consisting in the difference between their receipts and their payments to the State. Many of them were guilty of extortion. Most of them were rich, but hated and despised. When Jesus refers to a publican it is always in a tone of contempt.

Zacchaeus, then, was an influential publican. While he was trying to recognize Jesus at the moment of his entry into Jericho Jesus called him and announced his intention of lodging at his house. "When they saw it, all took it amiss; He has gone in to lodge, they said, with one who is a sinner [or as we should say, with a shady financier]. But Zacchaeus stood upright and said to the Lord, Here and now, Lord, I give half of what I have to the poor; and if I have wronged anyone in any way, I make restitution of it fourfold. Jesus turned to him and said, Today, salvation has been brought to this house; he too is a son of Abraham. That is what the Son of man has come for, to search out and to save what was lost."

Jesus does not tell Zacchaeus to give away the other half of his possessions or to impoverish himself, in spite of his frequent injunctions to give all that one has. But he perceives that Zacchaeus has yielded to a generous impulse; it is the impulse that counts, not the actual sum of money involved. It would have been just the same if Zacchaeus had offered one-third or two-thirds. It is the gesture to which Jesus gives credit.

We get the same impression from the parables, which are full of rich men who are sometimes symbols of the Father: there is the prodigal son's father (Luke 15. 11–32), the rich man who went out to hire labourers (Matt. 20, 1–16), the king who "resolved to enter into a reckoning with his servants" (Matt. 18. 23–35). This last is not only an image of God; he enriches the well-behaved servant. The parables, in fact, reflect a hierarchical and patriarchal society in which the rich are respected and influential, and in which everyone, whether rich or poor, is judged by his behaviour. If a rich man is wicked he is condemned, if he is good he is rewarded; but no judgement is passed on the social order. As we have already remarked, the Christian religion is concerned with the individual.

Not all the rich men in the parables are good. Two examples may be quoted. The first is that of the rich man (Luke 12. 16–21) whose lands yielded a heavy crop, who

decides to pull down his barns and build larger ones "to
store all my harvest and the goods that are mine; and then
I will say to my soul, Come, soul, thou hast goods in plenty
laid up for many years to come; take thy rest now, eat,
drink, and make merry. And God said, Thou fool, this
night thou must render up thy soul: and who will be master
now of all thou hast laid by? Thus it is with the man who
lays up treasure for himself, and has no credit with God."

The other example is that of the rich man and the beggar
Lazarus (Luke 16. 19–31). The rich man is clothed in
purple and lawn, and feasts sumptuously every day. The
beggar Lazarus lies at his gate, covered with sores, wishing
that he could be fed with the crumbs which fall from the
rich man's table. The dogs come and lick his sores, but the
rich man gives him nothing. Both die; Lazarus goes to
heaven, and the rich man to hell.

Certain contemporary non-Catholic writers have interpreted these parables as an attack on the rich as such, and
as a foretaste of socialism. Such writers, whose preoccupations are purely social, read into the Gospels a violent
social conflict. Christ's contrast between rich and poor is
interpreted by them as a class conflict, whereas it is in
reality merely the contrast between individuals. In the two
parables just quoted we are dealing with charity, not with
property.

Christ, we must repeat, was not a social reformer. He
passes no judgement on the distribution of wealth, he does
not criticize the establishment, he is not interested in con-
demning or reforming the structure of society. He speaks
to the heart. He takes society as it is, and requires his disciples to serve God and separate themselves from the world.
But he believes that riches are a hindrance to a godly life,
for "where your treasure-house is, there your heart is too".

CHAPTER III

CHRISTIAN COMMUNISM

THE FIRST COMMUNITY IN JERUSALEM

At the dawn of Christianity the first of the faithful, who founded the first Christian community in Jerusalem, adopted with enthusiasm a system of communal ownership.

> All the faithful held together, and shared all they had, selling their possessions and their means of livelihood, so as to distribute to all, as each had need (Acts 2, 44–5). There was one heart and soul in all the company of believers; none of them called any of his possessions his own, everything was shared in common... and great was the grace that rested on them all. None of them was destitute; all those who owned farms or houses used to sell them, and bring the price of what they had sold to lay it at the apostles' feet, so that each could have what share of it he needed (*ibid.* 4 32–5).

An impartial reading of this passage makes it clear that we are here dealing not with poverty, but with charity— "There was one heart and soul in all the company of believers." The saying attributed to the Pythagoreans, "Among friends all things are in common", is a commonplace in the literature of Greek social philosophy. Love is the basis of the Christian religion: the Lord is a lord of love, and sets an example of love. The disciples are spontaneously drawn to love, which to begin with takes the form of a sharing of life and goods.

This communal way of life was embraced voluntarily; it was not imposed by the apostles. It was a spontaneous demonstration of Christian brotherhood exhibited by an ardent band of believers. Moreover, this phenomenon recurs with the same spontaneity throughout the centuries, whenever earnest Christians are gathered together. I have witnessed it myself in student communities. It usually takes the form not of comprehensive lifelong associations, but of temporary associations for some limited purpose. Students leading a communal life generally have each their own family background. Their student life constitutes a part only, though a considerable part, of their whole lives.

The Jerusalem community is described in general terms only, the author's principal aim being to show how the Christians were filled with the spirit of charity. They certainly had their meals in common, but we cannot be certain that they lived together, nor do we know how they spent their days, or whether they continued at their trade or profession. We are not told that the apostles organized workshops or children's centres. "Communal life" must have been a relative term.

The relative and voluntary nature of this communal life is illustrated by the story of Ananias and his wife Sapphira, who sold an estate and brought a part of the proceeds to the apostles, pretending that it was the whole.

"Whereupon Peter said, Ananias, how is it that Satan has taken possession of thy heart, bidding thee defraud the Holy Spirit by keeping back some of the money that was paid thee for the land? Unsold, the property was thine; after the sale, the money was at thy disposal; what has put it into thy heart so to act? It is God, not man, thou hast defrauded" (Acts 5. 1–4).

It is clear that St Peter blames Ananias not for keeping

the money but for lying; and the falsehood is particularly serious for being in reality addressed to God.

The case of Ananias is interesting for us, because he is typical of the average Christian we meet today, living in a Christian community and open to demands on his generosity but unwilling to sacrifice either himself or his money. When moved to generosity, not from spontaneous love but from fear of offending society, he asks himself: How much ought I to give? Ananias considered that a part of the proceeds of his sale would suffice. His contribution may well have been greater than that of the others, for the community must have contained many poor men who had nothing at all to give.

Furthermore, as the case of Ananias may have already led us to suspect, a careful examination of the text suggests that communal ownership was only relative. St Luke begins by telling how all those who owned farms or houses sold them and brought the proceeds to the apostles, who then distributed them to all "as each had need", a proceeding which can accurately be described as radical communism. But he then goes on to tell how "a Levite called Joseph, a Cypriot by birth, to whom the apostles gave the fresh name of Barnabas . . . had an estate, which he sold, and brought the purchase-money to lay it at the apostles' feet" (Acts 4. 34–7.) The incident must have been striking for it to have been thought worth relating. The inference appears to be, either that landowners were rare among the early Christians—which is quite likely—or that those who sold their properties were the exceptions deserving to be singled out. Moreover, there is nothing to suggest that Joseph the deacon owned only this one estate. We may therefore conclude that in the preceding verses we have one of those generalizations to which an enthusiastic story-teller is prone.

ECONOMIC CONSEQUENCES

From the economic point of view, this experiment of the first Christian community proved a complete failure. The faithful sold their possessions, and the community lived from day to day on the proceeds brought in by its members. As we have seen, no attention was paid to production. This process of consumption divorced from production had the natural result of reducing the community to starvation and beggary. In the opinion of many modern commentators this improvidence was due not only to charity but to the expectation of the end of the world and the Last Judgement. The imminent end of the world removed the need for providing for the future.

However this may be, the community was rapidly reduced to destitution, nor has any other community attempted to repeat the experiment. In several of his Epistles St Paul asks for contributions from other churches for "the saints of Jerusalem" who have become dependent on their brethren.

In order to understand what happened we must remember that no Christian community was organized for production: as we have seen, Acts makes no mention of communal workshops. But to wonder at the early Christians' indifference to economic affairs would be to credit them with the outlook of our modern western civilization.

Even in our own day, the Arab world contains communities living in poverty, filth and idleness, and lacking any economic organization, who enjoy their life of indolence more than they suffer from poverty. The members of the Tuareg and of many other communities in the Near East are proud men, wearing their rags with great dignity, under-nourished, indifferent to production, but spending all their time in endless conversation, and preferring to talk all day instead of working to improve their standard of living. In some such way can we picture the early Christians living in a state of enthusiasm, talking interminably of the Kingdom of God.

Such a way of life would not be tolerated by men of the modern economic age. The whole existing civilization centres on productive labour. Capitalism and Communism are at one in holding that the end of life is the production of wealth. Furthermore, wealth is something which is *produced* by men's labour. It is the influence of the west which is propelling the whole modern world in the direction of this idea. It must never be forgotten that economic liberalism originated in England, and that the German Karl Marx lived in England. It is well known that the idea meets with resistance from the Arab and Indian peoples.

The economy of the ancient world was based solely on consumption. The fruits of the earth were regarded as a fund placed at man's disposal by God, and men lived on the bounty of nature, whom they looked upon as a kindly mother. No doubt there were limits to this bountifulness, and to overstep them meant destitution. The remedy applied was political, as for example when corn was shipped to Rome from Sicily, which was a political measure inasmuch as it was undertaken by the State. Nevertheless that was no general theory of production, nor did it occur to anybody to supplement the free gifts of nature by systematically using them for the production of further goods.

NOSTALGIA FOR COMMUNITY LIFE

However this may be, it remains a fact that the ghost of the communal or communist experiment carried out by the first Church of Jerusalem has haunted Christians throughout the centuries. This original community has constantly been held up as the perfect community, genuinely inspired by charity, the only society fully to have put into practice the charity of Christ.

The experiment has never been repeated, but at the same time no criticism has ever been brought against its lack of economic organization. When St Paul refers to the Church of Jerusalem and asks for help to support it, he neither criticizes the other Churches nor recommends them to follow its example. He warns the rich to "do good, enrich their lives with charitable deeds, always ready to give, and to share the common burden, laying down a sure foundation for themselves in time to come" (1 Timothy 6. 19). He does not tell them to sell and distribute their possessions, thereby reducing themselves to poverty. He himself was at pains to work for his living.

What we saw in the original community was charity. It was a society in which all things were shared, each member receiving "according to his needs", a formula now adopted by Communism and consequently unacceptable to Christians.

There are no grounds for supposing that the early Christians were enamoured of poverty. For them the emphasis was on the community spirit, which is the offspring of charity. Nowadays we use the terms communal and community because the word "communism" has been appropriated by social-economic theories of an anti-Christian tendency. The words have thus changed their meanings, and have necessarily acquired new shades of significance with the emergence of new problems unknown to the ancient world. The result may mark a progress in human thought.

Nevertheless, until the nineteenth century Christian thought has never ceased to be centred on the communism of

the first Christian community. There are constant references
to it in the Fathers. It stood for the golden age of Christianity. It is always spoken of as a model. No one ever
called attention to the fact that it was stillborn, and if
wherever there were Christians no Christian communities
were to be found practising complete sharing of possessions,
it was put down to the fact that all were lacking in the
spirit of Christ.

St Augustine says: "The first Christians employed their
private fortunes for the benefit of all. Did they by so doing
lose what they possessed? If they had kept their possessions
to themselves, each would have had no more than his own
fortune, each would have had only his own goods at his
disposal. But by sharing their own, they enriched themselves by the goods of others" (*Sermon* 113). As a matter
of fact, far from enriching each other, all grew poorer together; but at the time no one paid any attention to this
circumstance.

There is, besides, a confusion of ideas on this subject:
abuse of the rich is constantly mixed up with praise of
poverty and charity. The more logical modern approach
finds it strange that the rich should on the one hand be
blamed for being rich as if it were a crime, and on the
other exhorted to be generous in almsgiving, which they
could not possibly do if they ceased to be rich. On the
other hand, the feelings of the rich are worked on by
painting an appalling picture of the wretchedness of
poverty. Finally, there is insufficient appreciation of the difference between the idea of brotherly charity and the high
estimation of poverty. But the Fathers were not primarily
system-makers. For the most part they wrote sermons, that
is, occasional writings. The first attempt to treat the subject
systematically was made by St Augustine, but it was left

to the medieval scholastics to undertake the labour of bringing order out of confusion.

The earliest Christian philosophy was purely moral, and took no interest in theories of social organization. Again, it was not until the Middle Ages that Christians began to reflect on the problems of living in a society. It was then, too, that men began to study the rights of property and to speculate tentatively on economic questions. Following Christ's example, the early Christians were complete individualists; their approach to a problem was always personal. They spoke of rich men and poor men, and when they imagined a society containing neither, they could conceive of it only as a result of the practice of charity.

The period from the sixteenth to the eighteenth centuries saw the growth of a literature of Utopia which, though inspired by pagan Greek romances, was written by Christians such as Thomas More and Fénelon. According to these writers the ideal society is strictly communist—much more strictly than what we now call a "communist" society. From the nineteenth century onwards the anticlericalism of socialists has led to a breach with Christians, and today any Christian who still hankers after the ideal expressed in the formula "those who love one another hold all things in common" would prefer to express it by the term "communal".

After the period of persecutions the old spirit of Christian communism was re-born in monasticism, but in the form of an institution carefully buttressed by a system of elaborate rules. This we must now attempt to elucidate before dealing with the Christian's place in the economic system, a problem very much in men's minds today.

CHAPTER IV

CHRISTIAN POVERTY

There are a number of ideas implicit in the teaching of the Gospels which require clarification, for example the value of poverty (blessed are the poor), the dangers of wealth (it is difficult for a rich man to enter the kingdom of God) and the right use of natural resources. The two first are the most prominent, because they run most counter to man's natural propensities.

THE MERITS OF POVERTY

Poverty presents itself above all as a liberator. Worldly goods shut their possessors up in worldly desires and selfishness. They must therefore be renounced in order to follow the Saviour.

The idea of renouncing worldly goods is not the most original feature of the Christian religion: it occurs all over the world, in moderate form among the Greeks, the Cynics being more radical in their views than the Stoics and Neoplatonists, but in extreme form among the sages of the Far East. The originality of the Christian religion consists not in the idea of poverty but in the injunction to follow Christ. This idea is peculiar to Christianity, since obviously no other religion teaches that Christ is the Saviour. The good news that Jesus came to preach is that

God is our Father, and that through the mediation of
Christ we resume our relationship of God's children.
Consequently the originality of the Christian conception
resides not in the fact of poverty but in the purpose for
which we embrace it. In the sayings of Christ the injunction to sell all that belongs to us and give it to the poor
is nearly always accompanied by the injunction "Take up
your cross and follow me". The final aim and object of
human life is always to follow Christ.

It is a commonplace of the sages that one must detach
oneself from material things in order to cultivate the
things of the mind. But outside Christianity, it is usually
on *their own* minds that the sages fall back. Man is distinguished by his mind, and man is truly man only in so
far as he lives in the mind and devotes himself to the things
of the mind. But if we know nothing of God but his
transcendence, what object is there left for our devotion
but our own selves? In seeking God, it is still our own
good we are seeking. Christ, on the other hand, teaches
that God is our father, that his love for us is greater than
words can express, and that we are invited to partake of
the mystery of his fatherhood by becoming his children.
Christianity is steeped in God: God floods the universe with
love. We need quote no further texts: the whole of the
Gospel resounds with the theme of love. The Christian
religion is a religion of the divine.

We often hear talk of Christian humanism. Doubtless
there is such a philosophy, but Christianity is the religion
of divinity, not of humanity. It means that God is with
us, that the whole of human life is laid hold of and taken
over by God, and permeated by him. Indeed, if we are
Christians God is with us and in us, he is in everything
and governs everything, he is the lord of all. For a
Christian, life is self-surrender to God. Poverty sets men

free, and the object of this liberating process is that we should live our lives as children of the most loving of fathers. Only the poor are capable of such a life, because their vision is not obscured by attachment to worldly goods.

In Christianity asceticism takes second place to love. Asceticism means the conquest of self, from which it sets us free. The saying of Christ: "If a man strikes thee on thy right cheek, turn the other cheek also towards him" (Matt. 5. 39) is in the first place an injunction to mortify ourselves by self-discipline. Not to offer resistance to injury is usually sound advice, because it is principally by this practice of non-resistance that we assert our capacity for self-control. But a man cannot love unless he is free. When we love, our sole thought is of the loved one. For so long as we are thinking of ourselves, we are incapable of love.

It is at this point that the unique nature of Christian asceticism becomes apparent. It conduces not only to liberation from the desires of the flesh and subservience to public opinion, but to a forgetfulness of self which leaves no room in us except for God.

Now the Christian knows that God is by his side, ready to help him. He knows that God is within him, that God loves him with an unutterable love. For his part, he has only to throw down every barrier against the divine life within him to be filled with the ineffable majesty and love of God. None but the Christian knows this, for this is the gospel of Christ, and of Christ alone.

God is our guide. In the language of Christianity there is frequent mention of Providence, but to the man in the street it is only the pleasant things of life that are welcomed as providentially bestowed. In reality we owe everything to Providence and to grace: everything beyond the scope of our own free will comes to us by the will of God, misfortune

and trials no less than happiness. Or it may more accurately
be said that misfortunes are sent to try us. Every difficulty,
every obstacle in our path is placed there to provide us
with an opportunity to fulfil our human destiny and to
show what stuff we are made of. On this point, once again,
all philosophies are in agreement. But Christianity has
something more to add. Every obstacle, every difficulty is
a signpost set up by God to point the way he wishes us to
go. That is what is meant by Christ's saying: "Blessed are
those who mourn": blessed are those who have been put
to the test.

BLESSED ARE THE POOR

Poverty occupies a prominent place in the history of
Christian thought. In the Gospels man appears as a weak
creature for whom worldly goods are dangerous, in that
they tend to concentrate his attention on the pleasures of
this world, to the neglect of the Kingdom of God. Jesus
considers that his teaching will meet with a readier hearing
from the humble and meek than from the great ones of the
earth.

Here we must note the connection between poverty and
humility. Jesus constantly couples the humble with the
meek. Humility is that virtue by which man acknowledges
his dependence as a creature on his creator, and since our
creator is also our father, it is only by humility that we can
achieve the attitude of mind proper to a son, together with
the trust implied in the relation of son to father. The rich
and powerful trust in themselves, and feel no need to turn
to God for help.

The sayings in which our Lord calls us to renunciation
are couched in violent terms. We feel his conviction that
men will not find it easy to accept this teaching, and he

does not flinch from pressing it as strongly as possible, in terms which may even appear exaggerated. We have to bring about a reversal of values: since our weakness tends to make us forget God, it is salutary that our enjoyment of the good things of life should give way to what the world calls misfortune. Happiness becomes unhappiness, and unhappiness becomes happiness. It is a truth to which we are always coming back: the beatitudes—and the "woes" added to them by Luke—have no other significance.

Parallel with the teaching which, as we have seen, makes an early appearance in St Paul's Epistles and confines itself to enjoining generosity on the rich, we have already noticed another tradition which reviles the rich and praises the virtue and righteousness of the poor. In New Testament times this tradition asserts itself in the Epistle of St James:

> Is one of the brethren in humble circumstances? Let him be proud of it; it exalts him, whereas the rich man takes pride in what in truth abases him. The rich man will pass by like the bloom on the grass ... (1. 9). Has not God chosen the men who are poor in the world's eyes to be rich in faith, to be heirs of that kingdom which he has promised to those who love him? (2. 6). Come, you men of riches, bemoan yourselves and cry aloud over the miseries that are to overtake you. Corruption has fallen on your riches; all the fine clothes are left moth-eaten.... You have condemned and murdered the innocent man ... (5. 1, 6).

This contrast between the corruption of riches and the virtues of poverty became a commonplace of popular preaching and theology. Attempts were made to comfort the oppressed and the suffering by showing regard for them and offering them the hope of reward: they may be despised of men, but God loves them. The rich, on the other hand, must be made to feel uneasy in the pride of their insolent pleasure-seeking. The Fathers of the fourth and fifth centuries who, as we have remarked, were popular preachers, harp on this theme so vehemently that they have sometimes been branded as communists.

Two short typical passages may be quoted from St John Chrysostom. "Poverty is a sure refuge, a peaceful port, an abiding security, a joy free from dangers, a pure happiness, an untroubled life ... an abundance which nothing can assail" (*Cum Saturninus et Aurelianus*, 3) and "Is it not true that the rich man is swollen with pride, while the poor man is always humble and meek?" (*In Actis* 13. 4).

Sayings such as these, of which many examples might be quoted, strike us today as rather surprising, the reason being that since the social problem asserted itself in the nineteenth century, we have come to regard poverty as involving a great many disadvantages. On the other hand, now that abuse of the rich has been taken over by Socialist and communist writers and linked to anti-religious propaganda, Christians have abandoned the topic, and any Christian who adopted the attitude of the Fathers would immediately be suspected of being a communist. The communism of the Fathers was the subject of much study and debate up to the beginning of the present century, and it has taken a considerable time to place it in its proper perspective. Now that we see things more clearly, we no longer use the term "communism" which has been appropriated by Marxist communism, an anti-clerical and indeed anti-religious ideology incompatible with Christianity.

But neither the Fathers nor the Gospels can be understood unless we bear in mind that they are concerned solely with morals, and not at all with social reform. Society as they know it consists of rich and poor, and there is no question of changing this state of affairs. Since the poor are humble and the rich usually corrupt, it is to the poor that God shows his love. We remember the words of the

Blessed Virgin in the *Magnificat*: "He has filled the hungry with good things, and sent the rich away empty-handed."

On the other hand, it is noteworthy that the Fathers do not confuse poverty with destitution, from which it must be carefully distinguished. Poverty consists in the lack of superfluities, destitution in the lack of necessities. It is obvious that St John Chrysostom's poor man, in the passage quoted above, is healthy and comfortably off. He is neither a slave nor to be compared to the wretched serf of the Middle Ages, or the nineteenth-century proletarian, or the miserable under-nourished inhabitant of what we now call the under-developed countries. He is an unpretentious workingman of the artisan class.

To this class Jesus himself belonged. He was neither ragged nor under-nourished. The mysticism of poverty has led to great emphasis being placed on a few sayings in the Gospels, such as "Foxes have holes, and the birds of the air their resting-places; the Son of Man has nowhere to lay his head" (Matt. 8. 20). These sayings, however, are not intended to give a picture of the everyday life of Jesus; they are incidental remarks designed to teach the idea of renunciation.

This conception of poverty continued to be held up to the industrial revolution. We find it in La Fontaine's fable of "The Cobbler and the Business Man". The cobbler may be poor, but he earns a living by his labour; the business man is rich, but his life is poisoned by the worry of keeping or increasing his riches. La Fontaine is not preaching a sermon; the poem merely reflects the contemporary social system. It is in this sense that the apostles were poor men. They are often said to have been fishermen, and indeed some of them were; but they belonged to the artisan class. They were not destitute, and when Jesus visited Simon

Peter to cure his wife's mother there is nothing to suggest that Peter lived in a hovel.

Thus we see that the attitude which Christ invites us to adopt is to love poverty in the sense of working for a modest living. Moreover, we may deduce from his sayings that the "blessings" of the Beatitudes do not apply to a poor man who is discontented with his poverty, or eaten up with the desire to get rich. And the converse is equally true: a rich man, like Zacchaeus, who is bent on using his wealth for the benefit of the poor may be accounted "blessed". The Fathers, almost without exception, temper their diatribes against the rich by admitting that there are poor men who are "rich in spirit" and rich men who are "poor in spirit". These, however, especially in the second case, are the exceptions. It seems to be easier to reconcile the poor to poverty than to instil the spirit of poverty into the rich.

THE RICH AND THE SPIRIT OF POVERTY

This being so, how is it possible for a good Christian to be a rich man? For it seems at first sight as if no one is forced to be rich, and that it is the easiest thing in the world to cease being rich.

On closer inspection we perceive that wealth, like all other social advantages, is—as the word itself suggests— bound up with the social system. Wealth is a social not a moral phenomenon. It is connected with the formation of social classes, and particularly with that of an aristocracy. The wealthy class is the governing class, made up of landowners, industrialists, tradespeople and government officials. Rich people are to be found wherever there is a hierarchical society. This is a social question, and is therefore ignored by Christ, who took no interest in social questions. We shall doubtless have to deal with them when we come to discuss the economic system, but for the moment we are concerned with the moral aspect.

The social function of the feudal lord and the modern industrialist is bound up with wealth. The manager of a flourishing business is rich only in proportion to the success of his business, and the duty he owes to society is to make his business thrive. For an industrialist to hand over his factory to the poor would be equivalent to his going on strike. By giving up his possessions he would be shirking the duties imposed on him by society. Any unfair advantages he may enjoy can be abolished by social reform; but if a man is successfully performing an important task, he cannot justifiably be asked to abandon it. I use the word "abandon" instead of "renounce" because, in a case like this, renunciation would amount to desertion. It is for this reason that the Church has never required a virtuous king to renounce the throne.

Wealth is also bound up with the family. This is not the place to discuss the question of inherited wealth: suffice it to say that great inequalities of wealth are generally bound up with the right of inheritance, which is itself bound up with the institution of the family. If this institution is considered beneficial and necessary, its consequences must be accepted. Furthermore, although all the results of the hereditary principle may not meet with approval, its abolition would probably lead to the abolition of the family. This proposition, moreover, is supported by the experience of the Catholic religious orders, in which the attempt to establish absolute equality and poverty has demanded from their members the renunciation of all family ties.

What then does the spirit of poverty require of a rich man who retains his wealth? To Christ it is inconceivable that a disciple of his should *love* wealth for its own sake. It follows that the poor will not envy the rich, while to the rich their wealth will be a source of regret. They will appreciate that riches are a dangerous snare from which few are strong enough to escape. The rich Christian will seek an excuse for his wealth by putting it to good use, while the poor Christian will rejoice at being spared such an insidious temptation.

Consequently for the rich Christian the question is not "How much *ought* I to give? Am I giving enough?" Such a question implies an attachment to worldly goods, and a desire to hold on to as much as possible of them. The correct question to be asked is exactly the opposite: "Am I *obliged to hold on to* my possessions? How much *ought* I to keep?"

The rich young man in the parable was under no obligation to keep his possessions. The story mentions no social responsibilities which might have obliged him to keep up a rank in society. He asks our Lord what he must do to achieve eternal life, and Jesus replies: "Sell all that belongs to thee." But the young man dares not part with his possessions because of his attachment to them.

If you tell a rich man that he need not give away everything he possesses, he will usually experience a sense of relief. But Christianity, as we have seen, is an attitude of mind. What matters is not the material fact of wealth or poverty, but the spirit of poverty, which consists in *loving* poverty. Love of poverty is no formula: it is an attitude of mind, and God is not deceived. Jesus said: "Thy Father, who sees what is done in secret. . . ." The Christian lives in a personal union with God, a union of heart and soul. The man who keeps his possessions out of a sense of duty differs in the sight of God from the man who keeps them because he loves them, though outwardly the situation of the two is the same. But God sees what is done in secret, that is he sees into the heart.

Moreover, the outward behaviour of the two men will also differ. The one who regards himself as the "steward of the poor", and his possessions as capital to be invested in the service of God's kingdom, will behave very differently from the other.

The teaching of Christ is uncompromising: the reason why it is difficult for a rich man to enter God's kingdom is because it is difficult for him not to have his heart in his riches. Now attachment to riches corrupts utterly, for "You must serve God or money; you cannot serve both" (Matt. 6. 24). In the language of theology, love of money is a mortal sin, because it alienates the mind from God. At the same time we must insist that Christian virtue does not consist in *the fact* of giving away one's possessions—"I may give away all that I have, to feed the poor. . . . If I lack charity, it goes for nothing" (1 Cor. 13. 3)—any more than to be "poor in spirit" consists in the fact of being materially poor. Christianity is love, and only love. It is a spiritual religion, and speaks to the soul. Our deeds are important only to the extent that they express our feelings. The behaviour of the rich young man betrays his love of his possessions.

DEVOTION TO THE POOR

The conclusion is that poverty is a privilege while wealth is a danger, an attitude which is contrary to human nature.

We have remarked on the close connection between wealth and class. Membership of a particular social class involves the maintenance of a certain standard in dress, housing and food, which in turn presupposes a certain income, which is greater in the upper than in the middle class, and in the middle than in the working class. We are familiar nowadays with the prestige attaching to the white-collar worker who belongs to the middle class. The cost and standard of living are determined by the social class. Ownership of a bicycle or car, a wireless set or a bathroom becomes necessary if a family is to keep up with the neighbours and not, as they say in the east, to lose face.

Now it so happens that mankind pays more attention to such considerations than to any others. A feeling of inferiority in this respect leads to humiliation and concealment. The spectacle of genteel poverty, going without food in order to appear well dressed, is common to all times and places.

All sorts of excuses are commonly put forward in justification of this self-consciousness. Its causes are attributed to more than personal motives, as for example to moral or family considerations. Parents talk of keeping up a position for the sake of their children's future. Or a man will appeal to the demands, such as a certain type of house or make of car, imposed by his station in life. A business man will often consider it necessary for his prestige to own as large a car as his rivals.

There is a measure of truth in these arguments, but such as it is, it applies only to a man who is not a lover of money. That it does not usually hold good is obvious from the anxiety to keep up a position displayed by many people of neither breeding nor professional standing. The shame of poverty is the counterpart of the pride of wealth, the former being almost as widespread as the latter. But Christ wishes his disciples to rejoice in their poverty.

Moreover poverty, as we have seen, is connected with humility. Christ makes no discrimination between the poor, the meek and the humble. A Christian who belongs to the lower class rejoices in his origin and has no ambition to rise above it, whereas the Christian who belongs to the upper class regrets the accident of his birth. He may take pleasure in his opportunities for doing good, but he is aware of the tremendous risk and responsibility attaching to his privileges—or to what the world calls privileges! He envies the poor their spiritual freedom.

This is the explanation of that devotion to the poor which is one of the most characteristic features of the Christian religion. Nowadays this devotion has almost disappeared as a result of the growth of the Welfare State, of which we shall have something to say later on. But it played a great part in the early Church, it has left its mark on certain modern practices, and certainly deserves to be revived and adapted to contemporary conditions.

A whole book might be written on this devotion to the poor, although to the best of my knowledge no such book has yet been written. There is a frequently quoted sermon by Bossuet—what would nowadays be called a charity sermon—on the eminent importance ascribed by the Church to poverty, which does no more than repeat the teaching of tradition: the Church exists for the poor, the rich are admitted only in so far as they are the servants of the poor. It is among the poor that Jesus Christ is to be found.

Devotion to the poor—devotion and not simply charity —springs spontaneously from the awakening of the Christian conscience. It shows itself not only in the relief of poverty and of all forms of suffering, particularly sickness, but in a kind of cult of poverty as of sickness, inspired by the purely religious sentiment that the poor, the sick and in general the suffering, represent Jesus Christ, that what we do to the poor we do to Christ, and that our duty towards the poor is the same as our duty towards Christ.

This is the origin of, for example, the practice of many of the saints of entertaining the poor, and of the devotion to the poor exemplified by popes such as St Gregory the Great and kings such as St Louis. The only surviving trace of this kind of devotion seems to be the custom, still practised in the Maundy Thursday liturgy, of washing the feet of twelve poor men. In this connection there are two observations to be made.

In the first place, this devotion is directed not so much to benefiting the poor as to showing reverence for Christ. When an important personage entertains the poor and waits on them with his own hands, he is not seeking to make himself agreeable. His guests would undoubtedly feel less embarrassed eating by themselves in the kitchen. The same applies to the washing of feet on Maundy Thursday, which is not intended to give pleasure to the poor. This fact is noted by Sigrid Undset in her *Kristin Lavransdatter*, a tale of life in Norway in the Middle Ages. One of the characters in the novel makes a practice of entertaining the poor as distinguished guests, and another character points out that the poor are more likely to be repelled by such embarrassing treatment.

In the second place, devotion to poverty in no way implies love of poverty, in the sense of wishing to be poor. The rich respect the poor as representing Christ, but without necessarily wishing to become like them, for it is only in the sight of others that the poor man is Christ; he is not expected to take pleasure in his perfection, or to pride himself to others on being the image of Christ.

Thus devotion to the poor differs from that reasonable love of poverty to which Christ invites us. It is felt for the beggar, the tramp and the poverty-stricken. Like devotion to the sick, and for the same reason, it expresses charity towards Christ, and corresponds to a religious sentiment that embraces more than the individual victim of poverty.

It is therefore possible for the rich to show this devotion

to the poor without wishing themselves to be poor, just as one may devote oneself to the care and comfort of the sick without wishing to fall sick oneself. Poverty is here regarded as a misfortune, and it is because our Lord displayed a special charity towards his fellow creatures in adversity, with whom he identified himself in order to stimulate our own charity, that a Christian's devotion is extended to the poor. But this devotion does not prevent us from regarding poverty as a misfortune: rather the contrary, since it is by their misfortune that the poor command our sympathy.

Consequently a rich man's devotion to the poor expresses no regret on his part at not being poor himself, nor, *a fortiori*, does it diminish his desire to abolish pauperism, any more than devotion to the sick prevents one from wishing to cure the invalid, or from carrying on the war against disease in general. We shall discuss this matter later in the light of modern conditions. The problem of the abolition of pauperism did not arise in the ancient world, because no one in the then existing state of civilization could contemplate a reform of society which would guarantee the welfare of the entire population. We ought, however, to retain Christian devotion to the poor, since we shall have to consider whether it should not continue to be exercised under the new conditions of modern civilization.

THE MYSTIQUE OF POVERTY

Side by side with devotion to the poor there grew up in Christendom a cult of poverty for its own sake, whose devotees saw in poverty the essence of surrender to God. The Christian in love with perfection longed to be poor, utterly poor and so far as possible penniless. The lives of the saints are full of voluntary poverty.

No distinction was drawn between poverty and destitution: destitution was preferred, as constituting the last degree of poverty. The last degree of love and sacrifice cannot exist without the last degree of renunciation. The ideal was to possess nothing, in order to possess nothing but God.

Here it is no longer a question of the moderate degree of relative poverty associated with Christ and the apostles. Poverty seems to absorb the whole life of the Christian, and to become equated as it were with perfection.

This tradition culminates in St Francis of Assisi, the "little brother of the poor". The Gospel texts which preach renunciation of possessions assume such prominence in his eyes that poverty becomes the key to the whole Christian life. St Francis would apply the Gospel texts literally as they stand, *sine glossa* as he says: and the literal meaning of the Gospel is poverty. He was concerned solely to copy Christ's example exactly, and to his contemporaries he seemed a Christ returned to earth. Nevertheless, as we have seen, Christ did not live the life of a St Francis; he was neither a beggar nor dressed in rags, and there are other things in the Gospels beside sermons on poverty.

Whence comes this Christian concentration of the mind on poverty, of which St Francis affords so striking an example? In the first place, poverty is the means or the condition of total surrender to Providence. Poverty alone leaves everything to God, since if I possess nothing, there is no one but God to look after me. St Francis, in the well-known scene in which he returns all his possessions, down to his clothes, to the father he is forsaking, declares: "Henceforth I shall no longer say: My father, Peter Bernardone, but Our Father, who art in heaven."

Poverty is therefore primarily a means of relinquishing all possessions but God. God is our Father; in him we trust; every event becomes a sign of his will; never does our will come between God's will and our act.

In the second place, it is poverty alone that enables us to love our neighbour whole-heartedly. Every human conflict springs from the love of money. The poor man has nothing, and will quarrel with no one. Love of God and love of our neighbour comprise the whole law.

St Francis of Assisi marks a climax. Others before him had sought for God in total destitution, and the tradition has survived until our own day. But St Francis is "the little brother of the poor"; his life is symbolized by his marriage to "the Lady Poverty". Poverty brings happiness, because it commits the soul into the hands of God; it is bound up with humility. Jesus loved the humble and weak, and of such are the poor. The Franciscans were called the Friars Minor, a name suggesting humility and insignificance.

Only the poor can truly surrender themselves to God. And since money is the instrument of wealth, it is against money that St Francis fights with all the violence of his passionate nature. The Franciscan friars were forbidden to handle money; money was the accursed thing. If any one offered them alms, they were to let the money fall to the ground rather than accept it. Once when a friar accepted alms and put the money by, St Francis ordered him to lay it down on the asses' dung in the road.

The only thing that matters is to give oneself to God without reserve. If our life contains nothing but God, it will become a song of gladness. The spirit of St Francis is a mysticism of joy as well as of poverty. It is well expressed in the words "without reserve", which mean to reserve nothing *for oneself*, whereas money is something kept back, a means of becoming independent of God. When we give ourselves to God without reserve, God is our only guide. There is no longer any need to make plans. Every event

is determined by the will of God. We can live from moment
to moment, because God is in every moment. The Franciscan friar is God's vagabond, living and content to live on
whatever falls from the skies. His enthusiasm is fired by all
the Gospel sayings which bid him follow the example of
the birds of the air which never sow or reap, and yet the
heavenly Father feeds them.

We shall see in a moment that poverty has generally
been associated with the monastic life, but this is only a
matter of custom. The mysticism of poverty appears in
every place and in every shape and form, whenever a
Christian is concerned with complete self-surrender. Some
men, like St Roch and St Benedict Labre, have sought out
poverty by living as beggars, not subject to the discipline
of any religious order. In the nineteenth century St Joseph
Cottolengo founded in Turin a city of the poor for the
relief of every form of distress, based on absolute poverty
and subsisting on charity from hand to mouth. The cult
of poverty is constantly being revived, as an expression of
the Christian impulse to trust only in Providence, and as
a reaction against the universal tendency of men to assert
themselves by relying on material goods and material
security. The cult, as we shall see, still survives in new
forms suited to present-day conditions.

POVERTY AND MONASTICISM

Any account of the place of poverty in the Christian
life would be incomplete without a discussion of poverty
in the religious orders. This particular kind of poverty
has assumed such prominence in the Church that monastic
poverty has become almost synonymous with poverty in
general, and that most people imagine that there is no
problem of Christian poverty in the world at large.

The reason why the general attitude of Christians towards wealth and poverty was seldom discussed by the Fathers is that, in the last days of the ancient world, the specifically "religious" life was taking shape, and "religious" were becoming as it were specialists in poverty. The Fathers constantly referred to the problem as if it concerned all Christians, but from the Middle Ages onwards it is treated only within the framework of the monastic life.

In the last days of the ancient world theologians, taking their stand on the story of the rich young man, drew a distinction between precepts and counsels, and included poverty among the latter, since when we get the impression that the problem no longer presents itself to those who are content to follow the precepts. Since it is only the precepts that are universally binding, a refusal to follow the counsels cannot endanger the soul. The counsels constitute the sphere reserved to the chosen few who voluntarily undertake to follow them, and it is for this select minority that monastic life is organized. It follows that it is only within the framework of monasticism that the problem of poverty can arise.

We have already noted that in practice no such sharp distinction can be made. At all times there have been Christians enamoured of perfection who from various motives have remained in the world, where they aspire to that perfection for which the monastic life is the only conceivable model.

There is an enormous literature devoted to the monastic life, and to monastic poverty in particular. In every book dealing with the subject we find, alongside chapters on chastity and obedience, a chapter dealing with poverty. The monastic life is based on the three vows and the three virtues of poverty, chastity and obedience.

Historically, since the beginning of the Middle Ages the

problem of poverty has been discussed only by the members of religious orders. They are almost alone in writing on the subject of perfection, in which they are the experts. This is readily understandable when we remember that the religious orders were founded for the pursuit of perfection, and that they include the great majority of all those who study this question, whether as writers or readers. When, at the beginning of the seventeenth century, St Francis de Sales suggests that the laity should seek perfection by methods appropriate to their condition, we feel that he is an innovator, and his proposal was not taken up again until the twentieth century.

Poverty is therefore an essential, though not the only element in the monastic life. It is connected with the idea that a Christian, in his pursuit of holiness, should abstain from founding a family and from profiting from the status conferred by the performance of his duties towards society. The monk is not content with the practice of poverty: he renounces the world.

To begin with, there were two forms of the monastic life, the solitary or eremitical, and the communal or cenobitical. But the drawbacks of the hermit's life led to its gradual replacement by what is essentially a communal life. Now the monk is not satisfied with renouncing the world. He joins with other monks in a communal life which deprives him of his independence while guaranteeing him the necessaries of life. In the monastic life greater emphasis is laid on obedience than on poverty. In the Benedictine order, the oldest of the western orders, the monk vows obedience to the Rule, and poverty is included in obedience.

Monastic poverty is primarily a personal virtue, by which a man gives up worldly possessions in order to surrender himself wholly to God; and this renunciation is associated with asceticism, which aims to set the soul free by suppressing man's natural love of comfort and enjoyment. At the same time monastic poverty has a communal aspect bound up with obedience. The monk's self-dedication to God expresses itself in his submission to the Rule, and to his superiors who embody it. His poverty is necessary in order not only that he may place himself unreservedly in the hands of God, but also that he may be entirely dependent on his superiors. Obedience presupposes poverty.

On the other hand communal life guarantees the monk security. He gives up all personal possessions, since the sense of ownership and the acquisitive instinct are two of the greatest obstacles to the perfection aimed at in the religious life; in exchange the community must guarantee that he shall live his life untroubled by anxiety for the future. Such security is necessary for peace of mind: without it there can be no inner life.

Poverty combined with security means security in poverty. Peace is guaranteed on condition of renouncing the aims whose attainment is believed by the majority of mankind to bring happiness. Experience of the monastic life proves under what conditions a life of poverty may actually be lived, and demonstrates why such a life is beyond the reach of most men. The monk renounces family life, rank and social position, all of which are ties obliging him to hold on to his money or to worry about acquiring resources of his own. The facts are confirmed by the rarer cases of men like Benedict Joseph Labre who have pursued a life of true poverty outside the walls of a monastery. Poverty presupposes celibacy and complete freedom from all worldly duties. But these conditions do not and are not intended to apply to the mass of Christians. Jesus made no such demands on the centurion or on Zacchaeus.

Any man who considers it his duty to remain in the

world, to have children and carry on a career, must therefore take the consequences of his decision. He cannot dedicate himself to actual poverty. He should love poverty and approach as near to it as his circumstances permit, but it is impossible for him to achieve it completely.

We have said that in the monastic life poverty forms one element in a whole, and is counterbalanced by security. The poverty of a monk is personal; the community may be wealthy, and must possess means adequate to guarantee the security of its members. The female contemplative orders have always insisted on a dowry, because the community earns nothing, and must be certain of being able to maintain the nuns.

Nevertheless, there are disadvantages in wealthy communities. In the first place, they are misunderstood and give an impression of hypocrisy. Ordinary people find something false in the presence of poor monks in rich monasteries, and fail to see how such wealth can be justified. There is nothing to be said against a community whose modest resources barely suffice to provide an austere living for its members, but scandal is caused if a rich community occasionally indulges in extravagant expenditure. The feeling of uneasiness remains even when it is pointed out that the expenditure is incurred for church purposes or to provide a hostel for guests, and not for the welfare of the monks. The ordinary Christian cannot easily understand subtle distinctions, and suspects a subterfuge.

Moreover, collective wealth is a source of real danger for the monks themselves, who may be tempted to turn it to their own profit. In this case it is possible for a monk with no income of his own to live well at the expense of the community. Superiors may show greater or less generosity in calculating minimum requirements, and if they have adequate means at their disposal the amount is left to their discretion, with the result that a poor monk might be more comfortably off than many of the laity.

In the days of St Francis of Assisi there were frequent abuses, and monasteries were not generally regarded as houses of mortification. From the historical point of view, the contemporary situation explains the violence of the reaction in favour of poverty.

Canonically considered, the Franciscan reform does not seem of great importance: it went no further than the foundation of a religious order which renounced all property, whether collective or individual. But it would be a complete misrepresentation of the work of St Francis to confine it within these narrow limits. His concern was primarily a moral one, an attempt to carry out literally—*sine glossa*—the teaching of the Gospels, with the search for a recipe of total self-surrender to God.

Yet the history of the Franciscan order emphasizes once again the conditions under which a life of poverty can be effectively pursued. Once the friars became priests with the consequent need for study and the obligation of serving a church they were obliged to own monasteries and to possess a regular income. They have always kept something of the spirit of St Francis, but it proved necessary to modify the rule of absolute collective poverty.

CHAPTER V

CHRISTIAN POVERTY
AND TECHNICAL
CIVILIZATION

Our contemporary technical civilization has profoundly changed the conditions of human life. It is usual for attention to be focused almost exclusively on the industrial or economic aspect of this civilization. Economic liberalism as well as socialism have put forward the economic aspect, and production in particular, as being the outstanding features of modern civilization, and have gone so far as to make these two factors responsible for the whole system. Nevertheless, the question ought to be considered from a wider point of view, and attention paid to the innumerable repercussions of this civilization on all aspects of life.

We have no intention here of dealing directly with this problem. But since the changes brought about in modern life affect every aspect of human thought and action, the problems of poverty and of the employment of wealth must inevitably present themselves in a new light. All these problems are linked together. We shall attempt to separate them for purposes of analysis, but no one of them can be considered in isolation from the rest.

A CIVILIZATION OF PLENTY

The term Welfare State is frequently used to describe our modern civilization. This is an old idea which economists have always regarded as a goal to be aimed at. One of the most permanent traditions of universal ethics asserts that man's greatest blessing consists in having enough to live on, neither too much nor too little. The ideal society is defined as one in which there are neither rich nor poor.

What is there in this idea peculiar to our own civilization? The reason why it assumes such prominence today is that technological developments have made it possible to envisage a way of life so organized as to provide for the welfare of everybody. This ideal was expressed as early as the beginning of the seventeenth century when Henry of Navarre said that his ambition was that every Frenchman should enjoy a chicken for his Sunday dinner. But the reason why this saying was so frequently quoted was that in those days such a degree of affluence appeared to be unattainable. Today Henry's ambition is a commonplace of every political and economic programme. As things now stand, the possibility of universal prosperity has ceased to be utopian. Such a degree of prosperity presupposes a civilization of plenty. All social ideologies are based on the prospect of realizing this aspiration.

It may be said that Christianity holds a contrary view. It is undoubtedly opposed to our setting our hearts on material goods; it distrusts wealth. But we are now witnessing a reaction against the pitting of rich against poor. If Christianity mistrusts wealth, are we then to conclude that it favours an economy of destitution?

The question answers itself. It is true that poverty is to a certain extent an ideal, and that the violent hostility displayed by some ascetics to the love of worldly goods has led to their carrying the love of poverty to extremes; nevertheless, as we have seen, this is not the usual Christian view, nor does it correspond to the example set by Christ and the apostles. We have already pointed out that the poor, in the sense of the destitute, are regarded by the Gospels as unfortunates whose sufferings it is the duty of the rich to alleviate. It is bad Christianity to think that the Gospels require the poor to endure their plight, but absolve the rich from their responsibilities. This is an attitude constantly censured by the Fathers, and Bossuet in his sermon on the eminent position of the poor in the Church explains that the sole title of the rich to be admitted into the Church derives from the relief they bring to the poor.

Consequently, when Christ calls on the rich to get rid of their possessions so far as they can, he does not intend to reduce them to destitution. Destitution, which may be defined as a lack of the necessities of life, is no part of the Christian ideal. As early as the thirteenth century St Thomas was teaching that the practice of virtue requires a modest competence, and his teaching is confirmed by the tradition of the religious orders. It follows that destitution, which is an evil, must be distinguished from poverty, which consists simply in not being rich.

We shall return to this conception of wealth when we come to discuss the economic system. For the moment let us examine what is meant by a civilization of plenty.

The focusing of attention on plenty had the effect of turning men's minds to materialism. In nineteenth-century liberalism, and in the so-called market economy which has now succeeded it, this materialism took a practical form. It was held that the final end of life was to produce material goods, and that the way to produce the greatest possible quantity was by stimulating the acquisitive instinct. In socialism, and in its communist extension, materialism takes a theoretical form. It is held that in order to spur man on to master the material world it is necessary to destroy his hope of a life hereafter and his belief in spiritual realities, including not only the soul but God. These economic creeds raise in an acute form the problem of the Christian attitude to money.

When we come to discuss the economic system we shall find that for more than half a century pope after pope has striven to dispel the misunderstandings which have obscured this question. In any case, the Christian attitude is perfectly clear: all men must be guaranteed the degree of well-being necessary for their development as human beings. If some men are driven to carry the renunciation of worldly goods to the point of destitution, theirs must be regarded as a special vocation which, as we have seen, involves also the renunciation of many of the ordinary conditions of life and many of the obligations we owe to our fellow beings.

Nevertheless, a Christian civilization cannot be purely and simply a civilization of plenty. It must be a civilization inspired by charity and by the community spirit, all of whose members work together to grow more perfect in the love of God and of their neighbours. In such a civilization plenty should be a means to an end. To love one's neighbour without doing anything to ameliorate his lot is obviously not really to love him at all. It is equally obvious that modern civilization has the duty, as it has the power, to provide its members with a standard of living which will not hinder their spiritual life; but still this is only the means to the end. A plentiful supply of material goods is no more than a condition, though a necessary condition: it is no use preaching to a hungry man.

Plenty and comfort cannot be the end of social life. Here lies the danger threatening our civilization: by talking of a civilization of plenty we focus attention on the plenty as if it were an end in itself. The same holds good of the science of economics, which concerns itself exclusively with the problem of production and distribution, the object being to bring about an increase of wealth. There would be no harm in this if economics were content to study one department of life without claiming authority over all the rest; but nowadays this is clearly not the case. Economics claims authority over the whole of social life: the claim has been reduced to theory by marxism, and has been put into practice by those countries which adhere to the liberal tradition. All social phenomena whatsoever are attributed to economic causes, and social life is believed to have no important end other than the economic. As far as the civilization of plenty is concerned, this attitude results in making the end of social life consist in plenty, from which all other goods flow almost automatically.

It follows that a civilization of plenty, understood as one which makes plenty the sole objective of human activity, is profoundly opposed to Christianity, though it is true that Christianity stimulates men to improve their standard of living, not for its own sake but because all human virtue and progress depend on the enjoyment of a modest competence. Christ says that his disciples will be recognized from their feeding the hungry, clothing the naked and caring for the sick (Matt. 25. 34–40), and in response to this appeal Christian charities for the relief of every kind of distress have spread over the whole world. Consequently the Christian ideal has been rightly considered under three aspects. In the first place, the Christian despises money in so far as it ministers to pleasure and pride; in the second place, he uses money for the good of his fellow men; and in the third place, he pities the unfortunate and strives to alleviate their wretchedness, which he regards as true wretchedness; for poverty, or lack of money, is a very different thing from destitution.

But times have changed. Where our times differ from all past times is that we can now imagine a society so organized that no one is hungry, no one is naked, where sickness steadily diminishes and everyone is cared for. From the days of Jesus up to the nineteenth and even the twentieth centuries such a state of affairs was undreamt of except by the creators of utopias. It seemed inevitable and natural that there should be the rich and the poor, and that there should not be sufficient worldly goods to provide for all. The world lived in what we now call an economy of scarcity. We have now achieved an economy of plenty for the first time in history. This social situation has profoundly transformed the practical aspect of the problem of poverty.

It should moreover be noted that this transformation has only just begun. Poverty is still to be found in every country, even in the United States which are so proud of their wealth. Certain aspects of poverty have even worsened, as we see in the case of the waifs and strays, and in some negro quarters of the great cities. Over a large part of the world, in the so-called undeveloped countries, men still live as their forefathers lived. Yet there are regions from which destitution has been banished; and it might without great technical difficulty be abolished the whole world over, if men were virtuous and, in particular, if they practised charity.

If men were charitable! That is as much as to say, if they were disciples of Christ. What hinders the abolition of poverty is the lack of Christianity in the world. In former days the obstacles were technical: charity could do no more than relieve a state of wretchedness which technical means were powerless to abolish. Today the technical means exist, but they remain unused owing to the selfishness of the rich. The wealthy classes in their selfishness leave the poor in a state of destitution which they have the means to abolish. The wealthy countries in their selfishness abandon the poor countries to a state of destitution from which they might be rescued.

The popes have often urged that all the troubles of the world derive from the failure to apply the social teaching of the Church. There would be no communism if Christians had paid attention to the demands of their faith. But either Christians have not been Christians, or those who were were insufficient in number to take control of society.

This fact discloses an ambiguity in the word "Christian". When we say that Christians are not Christians, we mean that baptism into the Church and adherence to her outward way of life do not make a man a Christian in our sense of the term. He may no doubt be a Christian in respect of, for example, his devoutness and his domestic life; but his religion does not govern the whole of his behaviour.

The civilization of plenty poses two main problems, of production and of distribution. The first problem is that of providing everybody with an adequate subsistence, by which is meant one that will allow the development of their personalities. This problem may now be considered solved. Some countries have reached the point of taking steps to counter over-production, while leaving the others sunk in poverty.

On the other hand the problem of distribution is by no means solved, nor can it be solved on the basis of selfishness. To this problem the whole social movement of our times is directed.

It follows that the first duty of a Christian must be to aim at a system of distribution which will provide an adequate standard of living for all. It is not his duty to be poor, nor, if he carries it out, is he to be accused of gross materialism. It is a question of placing material things at the disposal of mankind to be used as means of self-fulfilment. Today whoever wishes to obey Christ's injunction to feed the hungry and clothe the naked must set to work on the social plane. Private charity takes second place to social planning.

STANDARDS OF LIVING

For the first time in history a comfortable standard of living is within the reach of all. In former days luxury was enjoyed by the privileged few. The means of raising the general standard of living were limited in the extreme. Once adequately fed and housed, a man had no other use for wealth than as a vehicle for display and a satisfaction of vanity. The rich built themselves vast mansions and palaces, sometimes left uninhabited, smothered in marble and gilding and painted ceilings. The palaces, for lack of adequate heating and lighting facilities, were cold and gloomy. These defects were compensated by a large staff of servants, easily recruited by the rich from the world of poverty surrounding them. The gorgeous clothes of the rich were often no pleasanter to wear than the rags of the poor, but they served as a mark of wealth. The poor man in his sheepskin was as warm as the rich man in his fur-lined coat, but the price of the furs was a token of the wearer's wealth. In the Gospels, whose background is a hot climate, the wicked rich are described as clothed in fine linen and spending their time in feasting.

Today life has been made pleasanter and easier by the

mass production of heating, lighting, transport and sensible and attractive clothes. These amenities are not so much an indication of wealth as a contribution to well-being. Nevertheless, amenities are expensive. Hence the overwhelming and universal desire for money to procure them. And the desire for money is as boundless as the supply of amenities is almost inexhaustible.

In former times an extremely wealthy minority enjoyed a certain extremely limited degree of comfort. Louis XIV in his palace of Versailles was worse off for heating and lighting than a well-to-do working man of our own day. He could summon his musicians to play for him at certain hours, but he had nothing to compare with the simple wireless set which brings music from all over the world to our homes.

Amenities have an irresistible attraction for the majority of mankind. They are the modern expression of the love of worldly goods, and they appeal to wider and wider social circles. The means to acquire them are so numerous and various that most people are obsessed by them. The desire for more amenities begets an ever-increasing desire for more money to buy them. There is a demand for smart clothes, for gadgets and mechanical appliances of every sort, for cars and refrigerators and radios. The more highly developed countries are no longer plagued with hunger, cold or darkness, and social customs are adapted to the benefits of civilization. The masses are thus under constant pressure to raise what is called the standard of living. The man who falls short of his neighbours' standards experiences a feeling of frustration: he becomes one of the have-nots.

When everyone goes bare-footed, lack of shoes produces no feeling of distress. When everyone wears shoes, shoes become a social necessity, and no one dares appear without them for fear of exposing his poverty-stricken state. No parents would venture any longer to send their children to school or go about themselves barefooted or even wearing clogs, unless they were employed in some trade where clogs have a professional significance. Nevertheless, shoes are a social, not a natural necessity.

But many countries have progressed far beyond the mere question of wearing shoes, and are concerned with much greater refinements of life. Where everybody eats meat and owns a radio, a bathroom and a refrigerator, the man who cannot keep up with the rest of the world feels he is a failure. Yet he is neither destitute nor even poor, except in a very specialized use of the word: he is merely "hard up".

It is possible to be "hard up" in the midst of plenty: all that is required is the failure to keep up with the neighbours. The old picaresque novels are full of aristocrats who starved at home in order to make a good show in public. But in those days this was a fate confined to a restricted class. With the rise in the standard of living and the exacting demands it makes, more and more people feel themselves to be "hard up".

The rise in the standard of living creates an insatiable and universal craving for material goods. Since most people can acquire only a part of what they want, they feel a sense of privation; for the joy of possession is less than the pain of having to go without what we want. The fact that the streets are lit up at night, and that we can travel by train or bus or underground railway, is no cause for rejoicing; but we cannot bear it if our neighbours have an electric iron or a car while we have none.

Only the exceptionally well off can afford all the available amenities, which is why the number of the discontented keeps pace with the rise in the standard of living.

At the same time the multiplication of amenities develops a craving for material goods more obsessive and widespread than has ever been known. A minority of thoughtful Christians have reacted by cultivating a new feeling for poverty.

A high standard of living is a source of freedom, comfort and enjoyment. When the means of heating and lighting are readily available, when we do not have to worry about getting enough to eat, when we have at our disposal a telephone, a typewriter, a rapid and efficient transport system, and labour-saving equipment for the home, our minds are set free to concentrate on higher things. A Christian who cares for spiritual values and is anxious to be of use in the world will make use of all these amenities.

But he will be their master, not their slave. They are means to an end.

Comfort consists in being well dressed and housed and heated. When there are ample means of enjoying and improving on these amenities, they tend to become a constant preoccupation.

Lastly, the facilities for enjoyment increase with the rise in living standards. Radio and television come to be thought of as indispensable amenities of modern life, while many of the machines which make life easier, such as a motor car, are at the same time sources of enjoyment.

All this has brought about, among good Christians, a reaction in favour of poverty and away from the gross materialism which goes with the preoccupation with comfort and the craving for pleasure, and leads to the selfish pursuit of sensual gratification. Here the problem for a Christian is to distinguish between what enables him to live on a higher plane and what swamps him in material things. In the French Christian family movement, for example, we find an attempt at discrimination, a search for a simple life not involving a return to primitive conditions. There is no going back to cooking on wood or charcoal, no cult of candlelight; gas and electricity are there to be used: but there is a reaction against the rage for more and better gadgets, for labour saving as an end in itself.

This movement gives rise to a number of practical problems. Take as an example a modern domestic invention. A refrigerator enables the housewife to buy food at long intervals and to keep it fresh. On the other hand it provides iced drinks throughout the summer. Now we ought not to reject an amenity on principle, owing to a kind of fear of life, nor ought we to pursue pleasure for its own sake, making it our main object in life. The problem is a delicate one, and is usually insoluble when it arises from an isolated case. It can be solved only in the context of a general attitude towards life which holds firmly to spiritual values, particularly charity, which puts the love and service of humanity before the pursuit of comfort, and, above all, refuses to make the pursuit of comfort for its own sake the sole end of life.

In short, this new spirit of poverty shows itself in a preference for the simple life. When a number of Christian families meet together for a common meal all are satisfied, and all are withstanding the temptation offered by indulgence in comfort and extravagance.

The indifference resulting from this attitude of mind causes no embarrassment, since it has a social character. It frees us from the tyranny of the environment. But it requires Christians to hold together. No individual is strong enough to go against the crowd: failure to observe the conventions stamps a man as an eccentric. Nowadays Christians who wish to live a Christian life must come together for mutual support against the pressure of the environment, and must cultivate those spiritual values which are alien to the whole trend of modern society towards comfort.

This new conception of poverty may also be linked to the virtues of moderation and sobriety, both of which are aspects of restraint. Comfort and well-being are neither to be sought for their own sakes nor pursued to extremes. Their value lies in the use to which they are put, which should be for the promotion of the spiritual welfare of mankind. The virtue of restraint presupposes a certain caution, a certain distrust of the temptations presented by material things. It calls for a spirit of reaction against the general trends of modern civilization. To be healthy, however, such a reaction must be more than merely negative: it must spring from a devotion to Christian values, all of which are based on charity.

EDUCATION

Another feature of modern society is the importance attached to education, as is shown by the fact that in all the so-called highly developed countries education is compulsory. One of the characteristics of under-developed countries is the number of illiterates.

Now universal education presupposes a certain standard of living. Children who grow up in slums or are undernourished cannot reach a normal standard of intelligence. There may no doubt be a reaction against the naïve view prevailing in the nineteenth century when universal education was beginning to spread, according to which education is sufficient in itself to foster virtue—"open the schools and shut the prisons". Nevertheless we all appreciate that education is a genuine boon to mankind, and that it is a means, though not the only means, of human progress. We recognize that it is a good thing, even if it is not a cure for all ills, and that without it man cannot develop his faculties.

Hence the immense thirst for education in modern society. In the most advanced countries education is compulsory up to the age of fourteen or fifteen, though most children remain at school even longer. In the under-developed countries thousands of young people willingly go without food in order to pursue their studies.

A sound education is impossible without a background of moderate prosperity. Here again, prosperity is not to be frantically pursued for its own sake, as if it were the source of all good. What is required is to provide human beings with a standard of living adequate for their development.

In Catholic countries the Church was formerly the chief promoter of education, and the school is one of the principal objects of her concern. This feature of modern civilization is thus in harmony with the attitude of mind appropriate to a disciple of Christ. But the modern world contributes a much clearer appreciation of the connection between education and prosperity, a factor which serves to throw an even stronger light on the importance of a social structure which guarantees prosperity to all.

HYGIENE

Another prominent feature of modern civilization is the importance attached to hygiene and medical care. The improvement of health is more than a matter of material well-being, though it is connected with the whole apparatus of technical and social progress.

The idea of hygiene is yet another of the fruits of a technical civilization. It results from scientific progress and from a more accurate knowledge of the conditions of health. By promoting physical fitness it enables a man to work harder and live longer. Longevity also is a characteristic feature of highly developed countries.

But there is a close connection between hygiene and the standard of living. Health is dependent on a satisfactory standard of housing, food and clothing. Modern science has made health a matter of public concern: we now speak of "public health" and "the health service". In former times health was a matter for the private individual: everyone looked after himself as best he could, and nothing was known of the principles of hygiene. Today we recognize the connection between health and the whole of life. The problem of health no longer consists in merely tending the sick, but in preventing the healthy from falling sick, and in seeing that everyone is as healthy as possible. As in education so in hygiene, it is now the realizable ideal of our technical civilization to provide medical attention for every citizen.

In its concern for health modern civilization joins hands with the Church, which has never forgotten our Lord's saying that his disciples would be recognized by their care for the sick. In this field, as in that of education, the Church was the first to attempt, with the means then at her disposal, to organize what we now call a health service, a sphere in which she still plays an important part. It need hardly be said that it is the duty of all Christians to associate themselves unreservedly with these activities.

Nevertheless, we must repeat, the Christian attitude will differ slightly from that of non-Christians, since health is no more an end in itself than general well-being, of which health is one item. Accordingly the Christian concern for health takes its place within a framework of preoccupations dominated by charity. The Christian is concerned to make men happy in the practice of virtue, and health is a prerequisite of virtue, associated as it is with that minimum standard of well-being without which, according to St Thomas, man cannot attain to virtue. But health by itself cannot, any more than education by itself, make men virtuous: neither good health nor a good education is inconsistent with depravity. For this reason it is an aberration of the mind to be exclusively obsessed with health. The same is true of the Welfare State. All material goods are means to an end, and ought to be considered as such: they may be necessary, but they are no more than means. Since they are necessary, we are bound to make use of them. It is the duty of a Catholic to adapt to existing circumstances the tradition of charity, of care for the poor and of the abolition of poverty; the tradition of education, care for the sick and medical welfare which is the Church's heritage. These traditions must be carried on under modern social conditions, and our technical civilization is capable of achieving far greater results than were obtainable in the past. But at the same time it is the duty of a Christian to incorporate these values in a synthesis which only his religion can supply.

FORESIGHT

The development of foresight in a technical civilization has assumed such proportions as to amount to a veritable revolution.

Yet foresight is the characteristic of man: it is one of the mental attributes by which he coordinates his actions towards an end. When man made his first tool he must have been looking ahead, for a tool is invented with an object in view which does not exist at the moment of its invention, but which already exists in the inventor's mind. Again, no one sows land without an expectation of the harvest to come. Everything that man does is based, in a sense, on foresight.

Nevertheless, in the conduct of everyday life, popular opinion has always admired thriftlessness and accused the thrifty of sordid calculation and inordinate attachment to material goods. We have already quoted the Gospel parable of the rich man who built great barns so as to be able to store his harvest, and we are all familiar with the sayings about the birds of the air who never sow or reap. It is always this aspect which is emphasized, although, as we shall see, there is another aspect which the Gospel does not overlook.

Moreover this idea of thriftlessness corresponds to an almost universal popular tradition. What is the use of saving and scraping when for all we know we may die tomorrow? In La Fontaine's fable "The Cobbler and the Business Man" the latter asks the Cobbler how much he earns.

> " 'Now tell me, Master Gregory,
>   What do you make a year?' says he.
>   'A year!' cries t'other with a grin,
>   'Why, Sir, that's not the way I count!
>   I can't afford to crack my wits
>   With totting up each day's amount.
>   I just hang on, and reckon it a win
>   If at New Year I find I'm quits.' " [1]

La Fontaine is here voicing the popular wisdom of the ages. I have never yet heard any criticism of this point of view; but it is strange that nobody today notices that the fable does not say whether the cobbler has a wife and family to be brought up, or why he does not wonder how he is to live when he grows old and is no longer able to work.

[1] Translated by Sir Edward Marsh, Everyman Edition, 1952.

Moreover La Fontaine in another of his fables, "The Grasshopper and the Ant", puts the opposite point of view.

> "A Grasshopper the summer long
> Sang her song,
> And found herself when winter came
> Without a morsel to her name."

But we do not go to La Fontaine for a system of philosophy. He is the voice of that wisdom of the people which has always recognized the two opposing principles.

On the other hand our technical civilization, adopting the mechanical standpoint, fosters the spirit of foresight. The improvement in machinery necessitates a more complex organization in industry, and there can be no organization without foresight. Thus we arrive at what is now called a "planned society". The whole of economic life is controlled by comprehensive plans which tend to leave little or no room for the inspiration of the moment.

In the next stage the exercise of foresight reacts on human values. The whole trend of civilization is in favour of foresight. The school-child must work every day for the end-of-term examination, which is itself the prelude to further study. Hygiene insists on our foreseeing the consequences of our behaviour. Dieting presupposes foresight, and central heating presupposes that one has decided on the method of heating when moving to a new house. A modern architect includes the position of every piece of furniture in his plans.

The next step is life insurance and insurance against accident for every worker. The modern ideal is for every young man to make provision for his old age.

Foresight is associated with security. The craving for security becomes a major social preoccupation. The whole life of society is arranged with a view to security, and the spirit of adventure which leads a man to launch out into life as the inspiration moves him appears more and more abnormal, even in a sense scandalous. We can no longer cross the street without wondering whether we shall be run over, we can no longer turn on a switch without knowing what the result will be. La Fontaine's cobbler is far-sighted in carrying out his daily job, but not in managing his life. Nowadays it is an understood thing that the happiness of the majority of mankind depends on their foreseeing everything and regulating the whole course of their lives from the cradle to the grave.

The working class movement is obsessed by the craving for security, and uncertainty about the future has become the greatest evil of working class conditions. It is no longer enough to earn a living like La Fontaine's cobbler; security is also an absolute necessity, and insecurity poisons life.

The modern mania for organized security shows itself not only in social legislation, but in the steady increase in all forms of pension and savings schemes and in insurance against death or accident. Modern man devotes an increasing proportion of his income to insuring himself against the unforeseen.

This development coincides with a movement which grew up spontaneously in the Church. We have seen that the tradition of the religious orders was to offset poverty by the guarantee of security, which was considered a necessary condition for the development of the spiritual life. Only a few exceptional individuals are called upon to renounce security and embrace absolute poverty.

Attempts are now being made to extend to all mankind, beginning with the more advanced peoples, this tradition which aspired to perfection while admitting that, even for a chosen few, perfection is unattainable without security. The attempt is clearly praiseworthy, and Christians are bound to lend it their help; but once again it must be subordinated to man's general mission in life.

In pursuing this ideal we become aware that the Gospel sayings contain as many condemnations as recommendations of foresight. Where want of foresight is praised we are in reality being enjoined to trust in God. Foresight is condemned in those cases where a man presumes to rely entirely on his own efforts, thereby demonstrating his refusal to trust in God. Christianity is essentially a religion of *personal* relations between God and man. The God preached by Christ is both Providence and Father, and man is in a constant and living relationship with him. On the other hand, man is bound to live the life of a man; Christianity is a religion of incarnation. The behaviour of a Christian is governed by human laws, and it is characteristic of mind to direct behaviour towards an end set up by mind.

In the parable of the talents, which occurs in both Matthew and Luke (Matt. 25. 14–29; Luke 19. 12–27), Jesus compares God to a rich man who, when he was going on his travels, committed a sum of money to each of his three servants. On his return, he praises the good servants for making a profit with the money, but blames and punishes the third servant for not doing so. The third servant is a bad servant. But how is it possible to make a profit without the exercise of foresight?

Elsewhere our Lord speaks even more explicitly. "Consider, if one of you has a mind to build a tower, does he not first sit down and count the cost that must be paid, if he is to have enough to finish it? Is he to lay the foundation, and then find himself unable to complete the work? ... Or if a king is setting out to joint battle with another king, does he not first sit down and deliberate, whether with his army of ten thousand he can meet the onset of one who has twenty thousand?" (Luke 14. 28–31).

Many more examples might be quoted, such as all the parables dealing with husbandry, with sowing and reaping, with the good tree that bears good fruit, with fishing, with the treasure hidden in a field: "a man has found it and hidden it again, and now, for the joy it gives him, is going home to sell all that he has and buy that field" (Matt. 13. 44).

The reason is obvious: foresight is in no way incompatible with trust in God. Moreover, the whole life of the Church is permeated with foresight. Canon law, the discipline of the sacraments, the rules of the religious orders— all these are calculated with a view to strengthening our belief in the supernatural. They are *calculated* in the sense that nothing is left to chance, that all is foreseen, that the goal is security. Indeed, the Church is sometimes accused of being too far-sighted, as in the case of nuns' dowries: but our Lord tells us that we ought to look ahead. The Christian ideal of perfection is to act like a man while at the same time trusting in God.

Nevertheless foresight, like any other moral virtue, requires to be exercised in moderation; it must not obstruct the virtues of vigour, initiative and enthusiasm, or the willingness to take the risks incidental to life. The Gospel indicates the golden mean by the emphasis it lays both on prudence and on trust in God. A healthy degree of prudence implies a capacity to run risks: the servant who made a profit with the money entrusted to him is contrasted with the servant who buried his money and ran no risks.

Now today we are constantly urged to look ahead. In the first place we have to calculate whether we can afford the many kinds of amenities waiting to tempt us. In the second place, insurance now bulks so largely in our lives that a young man of twenty hesitates to take a job unless he can look forward to a pension at the end of forty or fifty years: and if he does not himself take it into consideration his parents will put pressure on him to do so.

Against this attitude a reaction has set in which shows itself on the one hand in the popularity of travel books, and on the other in the lively revulsion against excessive prudence displayed by certain Christians, combined with an exaltation of the duty of improvidence.

It must be understood that what is being advocated is a healthy not a total improvidence. It does not rule out the rational prudence recommended by the Gospel, but it impels us first to consider the attractiveness of what we propose to do, and then to estimate our chances of success, and it allows room for that element of the incalculable which necessarily enters into the best laid plans.

In short, a Christian holds firmly by two principles: to govern his conduct by the reason which God has given him, and to show his readiness to meet the unforeseen by putting his trust in God. It was St Paul who compared the Christian to a competitor in a race: an athlete submits himself to a strict course of training, but on the day of the race he takes his chance.

THE RIGHT TO VIRTUE

We have now shown that a technical civilization offers to all men the conditions for development demanded by their status as human beings. But this development is bound up with a social organization which exerts increasing pressure as conditions improve. For the Christian, this human progress results in a flooding of the soul by the divine life, of which progress in virtue is the outward sign.

Virtue is nothing more than the condition and the manifestation of human progress in the proper sense of the term, and Christianity, the religion of incarnation, builds supernatural perfection on the foundations of natural or human perfection. For the Christian, the aim of social organization can in the long run be nothing else than to make possible the practice of virtue.

For men to *be* virtuous, it is not enough for virtue to be within their capacity; they must contribute, in addition, an inward, that is a personal attitude of mind. On the other hand, men cannot be virtuous if the necessary conditions are absent. Modern slum conditions afford a convincing proof of this proposition. Moreover, as we have seen, mankind has always had a more or less dim awareness of this truth, which has, however, acquired a quite new prominence in modern times.

In the present state of society it is the duty of a Christian to assert the right to virtue as the foremost of the rights of man. The rights asserted in successive declarations since the close of the eighteenth century, including recent international declarations, are valueless except in so far as they guarantee that basic right in which all the others are implied.

It is true that a few exceptional individuals succeed in attaining a high degree of perfection in circumstances of destitution and insecurity; but they are exercising a personal choice and obeying a special vocation. Moreover, these men of God have benefited throughout their youth from a training which has fostered that concern for moral purity which shows itself when they reach the age of maturity. They are not such an exception to the rule as might at first sight be supposed.

Wealth and a high standard of living are dangers to the extent in which they centre the mind on material values, while destitution, ignorance and insecurity are even greater dangers. The ideal conditions for men to practise virtue are to be found in a happy medium, when the mind is directed towards the values of charity and the service of God and our neighbour, and material goods are used as servants not as masters.

Nowadays there is a clearer distinction than formerly between poverty and destitution. Destitution is a hindrance to human development, as is wealth. Virtue resides in the enjoyment of a modest competence which allows a man to develop without exposing him to the ceaseless temptations presented by material and social pleasures.

Christians on the whole have perhaps not fully understood these problems. In their attitude towards modern progress they have wavered between blind infatuation and indiscriminate suspicion. Good Christians have sometimes given the impression of being hostile to progress, to the benefits of science, to foresight and planning and hygiene. The reason is that they have not always clearly perceived that all these things, though good in themselves, are only means to an end, that they do not constitute the sole and final end of man, that they are to be used only for some ulterior purpose. If the whole body of Christians were to follow the reiterated teaching of the Church in her ringing affirmation of virtue as the most fundamental of the rights of man, and if they would show themselves ready to welcome everything that exalts mankind by upholding virtue, they would play a part in the world as catalysts of every kind of progress.

CHAPTER VI

COMMUNITY OF

INTENTION

So far we have confined ourselves to the moral aspect of our problem, the only aspect dealt with by Christ. We must now turn to the social problem.

Morality is concerned with individual acts. "What must I do?" was the question put to Christ by the rich young man. The social problem is the problem of communal organization: how should society be organized to enable man to achieve his end? The moral problem of money is to know whether we ought to love money. The social problem of money is to know how to distribute it in such a way as to enable man to achieve his end.

We have found it impossible to discuss the problem of modern technical civilization without touching on the social problem; the time has now come for us to deal with it directly. The Christian's attitude towards the social problem of distribution is based on his conception of human relationships, and on the value which he attaches to worldly goods.

THE BROTHERHOOD OF MAN

The brotherhood of man, like the fatherhood of God of which it is the counterpart, is one of the fundamental truths of the Christian religion. Men are brothers because they are all sons of one Father.

We have already shown what a wealth of meaning is contained in the Christian idea of the fatherhood of God. The brotherhood of man is no more an abstract theory than is the fatherhood of God. God is our Father in the most real, the most existential sense of the word. He is more our father than is our physical father. In the language of philosophy we might say that God is essentially our father, while our physical father is our fortuitous father (*per accidens*). I am who I am, because I am the son of a particular man and a particular woman, to whose encounter at a particular moment I owe my physical existence. But all this came about only because God is the author of all things, because he created the world as he created it, and keeps it in being from one moment to another. God is in everything that happens; he is in everything that I am, and in everything that each one of us is. Everything comes from him, and everything belongs to him.

We are brothers because we are all sons of God, and the brotherly relationship between men is a much closer and stronger tie than the subsidiary ties uniting narrower groups such as the family, the class or the nation. All men belong to the same family: Christianity does not speak of solidarity or citizenship but of brotherhood, and the tie of brotherhood is the strongest of all. Any Christian who fails to demonstrate the strength of this relationship is not true to his faith.

Moreover, worldly goods are family goods. Reverting to the terms used above, we may say that all goods belong essentially to God, and only in a subsidiary way to man. God entrusts them to man to be used in accordance with his will. They remain his property. He is Father, Creator and Lord. The first and basic question to be asked about goods is for what purpose God intends them to be used.

My personal right to them is a minor and subordinate question.

COMMUNITY OF GOODS ASCRIBED TO THE NATURAL LAW

This title is taken from St. Thomas (*Sum. Theol.* IIa IIae, Q. 66, *art.* 2, *rep.* 1) whose system of philosophy carries authority in the Church. However, the words quoted do no more than repeat what has always been the Church's traditional teaching.

As we have just seen, it is to God that all things belong. God places the fruits of the earth at man's disposal, but he is their sole dispenser: man has no right to dispose of them otherwise than in accordance with God's will. All things come from God, all things depend on God.

In placing the world at man's disposal God has no other purpose than that man should serve him. In order to serve God, man must begin by self-development, by perfecting in himself all the specifically human qualities. Human life, it must always be remembered, consists in serving God, in devoting one's life to helping one's fellow men to build a brotherhood of man. In setting ourselves this task we must never overlook that half of the human race which is still under-nourished and riddled with disease, existing side by side with certain other peoples or classes which are bursting with prosperity.

Thus we see that God places the resources of nature at the disposal of men, of all men. All should be able to live on these resources, and if they are not enough for all, at any rate as many as possible ought to be enabled to enjoy them. A rich man who has everything he wants while his poor neighbour is in need is a criminal. A rich country nowadays which has a surplus while its neighbours are in want is a criminal. Every individual citizen who does not scruple to take advantage of his belonging to such a country is also a criminal and deserving of punishment.

No lesson is more constantly reiterated in the tradition of the Church. It is exactly expressed in the words of the *Code social*: "Material goods are essentially ordained for the requirements of the human race and of all mankind. This common purpose, however, does not forbid their private or personal ownership, which is in accordance with human nature and advantageous to the order of society. Under whatever system of ownership, the primary purpose of material goods must be safeguarded" (*Art.* 101).

We shall have more to say later about ownership: for the moment we are concerned with the question of principle. It is a principle which is constantly cropping up. Within our own lifetime it has been frequently dealt with by the popes, and it has been increasingly emphasized in the course of the present century. Leo XIII made only a passing allusion to it in *Rerum Novarum*, but Pius XII reverted to it whenever he discussed ownership. Again, it is in connection with ownership that St Thomas lays down the principle.

Nevertheless, this principle is usually dismissed in a sentence, whereas pages are devoted to the question of private property. The reason for this at first sight surprising treatment will appear later. For the moment, all we need say is that the general principle is left undiscussed owing to its very obviousness, to which the whole of Christian philosophy bears witness. This is often the fate of self-evident principles: they are thought to require no proof. The reason why fuller treatment is accorded to the right of ownership is that no self-evident principle is here involved, ownership being lawful only in certain circumstances which require to be defined.

For a discussion of principles we must go back to the

Fathers. We have already seen that they lived in a society where the rights of property gave rise to numerous abuses, unaccompanied by any discussion of principles. The Fathers accordingly reacted violently, often reminding the rich that they were responsible in the sight of God for the way they used their wealth, and that the poor had a claim on the goods appropriated to themselves by the rich.

Out of many passages on this theme we may first quote from St John Chrysostom, the most outspoken of them all.

> God has given us the sun, the stars, the heavens, the rivers, all of which we enjoy in common, none of which is for our private use, nor do they call for any expenditure or labour on our part. This is nature's law and image. Now if God gave all these things for our common enjoyment, his purpose undoubtedly was to teach us to possess all other things in common.
>
> It is because a few men attempt to appropriate to themselves what belongs to all that disputes and wars break out, as if nature were outraged that man, with his chilly "yours" and "mine", should import division into the unity ordained by God ... (*In 1 Tim.*, hom. *12*). These words "yours" and "mine" have no meaning whatever. ... In calling a house "yours" you are talking nonsense. The air and the earth belong to the Creator, and all dwellings together with their builders, and all other things without exception. (*In 1 Cor.*, hom. *10, 3*).

In more moderate terms St Ambrose also deals with the same theme:

> It was for the common use of all men, rich and poor, that the earth was created. Why then do you rich men claim for yourselves a monopoly in the ownership of land? Nature knows nothing of rich men. All her children are born in poverty and nakedness, and bring with them into the world neither gold nor silver. ... The alms you give to a poor man are not yours to give: you are restoring to him a portion of what is his own, for what you have appropriated

to your own sole use was created for the use of all. The
earth belongs to all, not to the rich alone (*De Nabuthe
Jezraelita* 1, 2 and 3). . . . The Lord God ordained that this
earth should be the common possession of all men, and
that its fruits should be enjoyed by all: it is greed that
has engendered the rights of property (*In Ps. 118*, 8. 22).

In later times it was on the right of ownership that
attention was focused, and men were content to recall the
general principle of what might be termed the original
common ownership of goods. Hence arose the formula
which has become classical in Christian social philosophy,
according to which goods are public by intention but private by use; in other words, that private ownership is the
best means of placing goods at the disposal of the public.
Nevertheless, underlying this doctrine is the general idea
that goods are intended for the benefit of all.

We remarked above that Pius XII laid more stress than
did his predecessors on the idea that "the dignity of
human personality normally requires, as the natural basis
for living, the right to make use of natural resources"
(Christmas message of 1942). These sentiments are deliberate, and due to no personal preference on the part of
Pius XII, whose utterances were always directed to re-
calling the unchanging tradition of the Church and the
exact bearing of the Christian message. With the passage
of time, however, certain aspects of that message have
acquired a new prominence.

THE TRADITIONAL DOCTRINE

For the purpose of forming an accurate idea of the Christian tradition it is advisable to go back to the Middle Ages,
and in particular to St Thomas who gave it its most comprehensive formulation. The Fathers of the Church, as we
have seen, were preachers and moralists. They were not
concerned with social theory, and it is only by singling out

a few isolated passages that we can arrive at their implicitly held beliefs. On the other hand, the medieval writers were members of a Christian society and professional teachers. They were more systematic thinkers and, although primarily theologians and moralists, found themselves under the necessity of dealing with the social question. It is in connection with theft that St Thomas justifies property, since theft is a sin only if property is lawful. At the same time these writers, being primarily moralists, are led to discuss the duty of the citizen and the function of the State, or the Ruler. On the other hand their study of the problems of charity and justice leads them also to take into consideration the duty of every individual.

But the medieval writers had the advantage over us in that they lived among Christians in a Christian society, in which the search for the principles of action might be conducted without the necessity of constantly referring to pagan theories, towards which a Christian is obliged to define his attitude. In this respect liberalism in its economic applications, and socialism, principally in its marxist form, have brought about a worsening of the situation. For the last one hundred and fifty years these two doctrines have monopolized the political and social scene, and the antagonism between them has governed almost the whole conduct of public affairs. As a result of the importance they have assumed it has become impossible to approach any social problem without first taking sides.

We need not consider why, in this field, Catholics have remained in the background for more than a century. Even today many of them are content with ideas put forward by non-Christians, and demonstrate their faith only by asking what they ought to think of these doctrines: it never occurs to them to formulate a sociology of their own based on their Christian beliefs. Now we have seen that Christianity is first and foremost an attitude of mind, a way of thinking and living. Christians who adopt a theory inspired by an alien attitude of mind will at once find themselves in an impossible situation.

This is exactly what has happened. Liberalism and marxism have stolen the limelight, and have either directly or indirectly contaminated the minds of a great many Catholics. The questions under discussion threaten to subvert the Christian tradition at several points: the Church therefore intervenes in defence of the faith. The reason for the many papal pronouncements on social problems during the last century is the danger threatening the Christian heritage in this field.

The teaching of the Church takes two forms, reminding us of the tradition and applying it to contemporary conditions; but it is this second aspect which prompts her intervention. If the tradition were not threatened, there would be no need for the popes to recall it to mind. It follows that the encyclicals are a kind of "occasional writings", in the sense that papal intervention is prompted by present-day circumstances: they deal with controversial questions of the day.

Now contemporary controversy turns not on the general Christian attitude towards money, but principally on the problem of labour arising from the growth of capitalism, as well as on the rights of property and the function of the State. Consequently it is in connection with these questions that the Church addresses herself to social problems. For this reason, if we wish to think calmly about the problems under discussion, we should do well to go back to a time when they presented themselves to Christians in what we might call a "pure" form, unobscured by false perspectives and false attitudes of mind.

Most Christians find it hard to realize to what an extent the theories of liberalism and marxism are literal monstrosities, in that they completely distort reality by extrapolating certain of its aspects, which they isolate while claiming that they form the whole basis of the social order. The popes have constantly warned Christians against this tendency, but in so doing they have been led to overstress the points on which these theories have, we repeat, laid a monstrous and distorting emphasis. On the other hand, these theories are closely connected with the anticlericalism now in vogue, and are the open or underhand enemies of religion. In the midst of the seething conflict of ideas and emotions the teaching of the Church shines like a beacon; yet there are many who fail to perceive the connection between the *ad hoc* pronouncements of the Church and the main body of the Christian tradition. A reference to the tradition prevailing in less troublous times will throw light on a number of contemporary points of view.

St Thomas, like all the old writers, wrote at a time when society was largely based on property. Property was both political and economic, that is, the landowner was both a rich man and a nobleman. We have already remarked, in one quotation from St Ambrose, that in those days property consisted mainly in land. Personal property was not yet of any importance, and is referred to only incidentally by contemporary writers. The great landowner was lord both of the land and of the peasant who lived on it.

Now possessions were intended for the community. It was considered advisable to determine their ownership in accordance with individual property rights, but as regards their use, "man ought to possess external things, not as his own, but as common, so that, to wit, he is ready to communicate them to others in their need" (*Sum. Theol.* IIa IIae, Q. 66, *art.* 2). Elsewhere St Thomas adds that we sin against our fellow men by not allowing them to avail themselves of our goods (*ibid.* Q. 119, *art.* 3, *ad* 1). The first of the passages quoted above was taken up by Leo

XIII in the encyclical *Rerum Novarum* and by Pius XI in the encyclical *Quadragesimo Anno*.

On this point, to which he frequently recurs, St Thomas is adamant. Referring to the statement of St Ambrose "Let no man call his own that which is common property" he says: "He is speaking of ownership as regards use, wherefore he adds: *To spend more than enough is to take by violence*" (*ibid*. Q. 66, *art*. 2, *ad* 2).

Notice that St Thomas uses the word *ought*. This is not a question of appealing to the generosity of the rich: they have a duty to perform, and anyone who shirks it is a criminal.

This conception of the employment of wealth is based on a general conception of life in society. St Thomas does not object to the rich as such, because he does not envisage any other form of society. But he agrees with the Fathers in holding the rich responsible for their wealth with respect to their neighbours, who are the poor. In the social conditions then prevailing, charity was the sole means of ensuring to the poor a share in the wealth of the rich. It is a question of means, and from this point of view we shall see that the situation today is different.

It should, however, be added that, in St Thomas's view, the bond of society commits the whole man to the service of the community: he is accountable to the community not only for himself and his actions but for all his possessions. Moreover, service to the community is equated with service to each one of its members. Society is composed of interdependent individuals, and has for its object the development of each one of its members, both collectively and individually. No community can be perfect unless its members are perfect. When we strive to perfect ourselves we are striving for the common good, and in striving for the common good we are striving for our own benefit. In dealing with this subject, St Thomas employs general phrases which go beyond the concept of charity. "When a man is a member of a community, he is at the service of that community (*qui servit alicui communitati*) and, by that very fact, at the service of every one of its members" (*Sum. Theol.* Ia IIae, Q. 58, *art.* 5).

This is an idea never far from St Thomas's thought. He constantly repeats that the individual exists by his very nature for the sake of the community, and if this is true of his person, it must *a fortiori* be true of his possessions. Therefore, he who denies to the community the use of his goods is a criminal. A number of conclusions may be drawn from this proposition. Cajetan, in his commentary on St Thomas (*Sum. Theol.* Ia IIac, Q. 118, *art.* 4, no. 3), explicitly asserts that if a rich man refuses to share his superfluous possessions, the judge is officially entitled to distribute them among the needy, even apart from cases of extreme necessity, in order that justice may be observed.

"According to the teaching of the saint, superfluous wealth is granted to the rich only that they may acquire merit by distributing it fairly. . . . Consequently they wrong the needy by refusing to distribute their superfluity: and it is this injustice that the ruler, who is the upholder of justice, can and must put right, so soon as the fact is patently established."

This passage goes much further than the diatribes of the Fathers. The latter contented themselves with exhortation: they upbraided the rich for behaving unjustly, but confined themselves to trying to convert them, and did not contemplate taking legal action against them if they failed to carry out their duties. Cajetan himself takes the legal standpoint, and with professorial calm maintains that a rich man failing in his duty may be deprived of his possessions. No one has gone to such extremes in any civilized society. St Thomas says that the ruler performs his duty when "he corrects what is out of order, supplies what is lacking, and improves what can be improved" (*On the Governance of Rulers,* I, chap. 15).

There is no question of restricting the power of the ruler, whose function it is to secure the welfare of his subjects, and to watch over the public interest: that, and no more.

THE TWENTIETH-CENTURY ECONOMIC SYSTEM

It need scarcely be said that no rich man has ever lived up to St Thomas's ideal, that no court of law has ever taken the action recommended by Cajetan, and that no ruler has ever played the part assigned to him by St Thomas.

If, from time to time, a rich man is found to be virtuous, he may earn a blessing from the poor, but he is usually regarded with suspicion by his fellows: a virtuous judge will be checkmated by the powers that be, and a virtuous ruler will find his best intentions thwarted by his entourage: he may even, if the necessity arises, be put to death like Charles the Good, Count of Flanders, in the twelfth century.

But today a change has come over the scene. The scientific age in which we live has transformed the conditions of life for the whole of mankind.

In the first place, the very idea of natural resources has changed its meaning. When the ancients declared that natural resources were placed by God at the disposal of mankind, they were referring almost solely to a part of what are now called "raw materials". We say "a part of", since we are dealing almost exclusively with the products of the earth's surface, there being at that time no means of exploring the depths of the subsoil. We remarked that for St Ambrose property was essentially landed property, and his view is shared both by St Thomas and by the authors of the French Civil Code of 1804. It is the industrial revolution and the development of technology that have brought about a change in the situation.

The old ideas reflect a society in which mankind had at its disposal very little more than the natural products of the earth. No doubt human industry could add something, but not very much. Nature made the greater contribution unassisted by man, which accounts for the religious conception of all things being placed at man's disposal by God, man not being the creator of the natural world.

But with the growth of technology, nature's contribution becomes restricted to supplying the raw materials for man's industry, which has discovered a large number of raw materials unknown to the ancients. More and more of the materials used by man for food and clothing are finished products, very different from natural products, such as fertilizers, tinned fruit and vegetables, and nylon fabrics. In other words, the materials employed by man in his daily life are coming to depend more and more on his labour: natural products are gradually displaced by man-made products. It is no longer felt that man merely enjoys the fruits of the earth bestowed on him by God: it seems as if man himself were the author or the creator, or at least the agent, of his own well-being.

It remains as true as ever it was that all these good things come from God, but in a more indirect manner. They come from God because God is the creator of man as well as of the natural world: it was God who bestowed on man the mind and muscle without which he can do nothing. But man is no longer content, as he once was, with the bare statement that all material things are placed at his disposal by God. What man receives from God is not only material things but also his mental and physical endowments, to the end that he may use material things for the building of a new world stamped with the mark of his intelligence.

In our industrial age there is an increasing tendency for men to become more important than natural resources. The rich countries are the hard-working countries. For example Switzerland and Belgium, which are almost entirely lacking in natural resources, have succeeded in becoming two of the richest countries in the world owing to the industry of their inhabitants.

But in proportion as civilization adds to the resources at man's disposal, labour becomes a cooperative undertaking, and cooperation plays an increasingly important rôle. At the same time, man's activities become interdependent, and social activities become communal activities, with the result that wealth comes to depend on the general activity of the community and on its organization. The principal problem confronting the economic system becomes that of production. Next comes the problem of distribution.

When all undertakings are cooperative it becomes difficult to determine the individual's share in production. Even the apparently most natural undertakings, such as agriculture, owe their success to the social organization. In a civilized country the farmer buys his seed and fertilizers from abroad, obtains his machinery from industry, and can sell his product only at the general market price. Universal cooperation implies universal centralization, under the control either of the State or of increasingly powerful combines. The individual is powerless to act by himself.

Since the value of goods is derived principally from labour, labour becomes also the principal source of prosperity, and we are no longer concerned solely with private individuals working for themselves, but with organized labour. Since organization is essential, the part played by management continues to increase, and management, or the direction of economic life, becomes the main problem of economics.

Thus the economic problem is one of production and of distribution, both of which are essentially collective enterprises, concerned with producing and distributing for the greatest benefit of the community. It is the duty of every individual to shoulder his share of the common task, a task in which all must cooperate, but from which all must benefit and gain a living.

It is at first sight surprising to find, in modern works on economics, no chapter dealing with ownership, the reason being that the chief problem in our days is that of management. It matters little who owns a business: if it is badly managed or not managed at all, it will be unproductive, whereas under management, even other than the owner's, it becomes productive. Hence the first problem exercising the economists is that of sound management. But sound management ought to benefit all who take part in economic activity.

Economists are concerned with the promotion of the common weal. They may differ over the means to be employed, but all are agreed on the objective. Goods constitute a stock raised by collective industry, and this collective industry ought to promote the prosperity of the community as a whole. Goods are communal by intention.

Thus the primary aim of economic activity is to produce goods in sufficient quantity to provide an adequate standard of living. Such a standard includes not only food and clothing but educational and health services, together with the security which is itself dependent on the social organization. The total resources make up a fund from which the individual draws what he requires according to his income. The total incomes make up the national revenue, which is a fund to be laid out for the common weal.

This whole conception is no more than a reversion to the ancient idea that the totality of goods is available to the totality of men; in its modern form, however, it has parted from its basis in religion, and appears in such a novel guise that the original doctrine underlying it is barely recognizable. When modern economists base their science on the concepts of national income or net national productivity, they fancy they are saying something quite new. As a matter of fact it was only in the nineteenth century that these concepts were accepted as fundamental and passed into current use. Before that time, incomes were thought of as essentially private incomes. The liberalism which triumphed with the extending influence of the commercial and industrial classes regarded the owner as sole master of his property, accountable to no one. Today the rich feel the need of justifying themselves by pleading the services which they render to the community.

All these factors have brought about a change both of attitude and of vocabulary. But the traditional view still holds good that the totality of goods is at the disposal of the total population.

The distribution of the national income is effected in innumerable ways which are the result of the different types of social structure, and also of the clash of interests which arises when every individual pursues what he considers he is entitled to, or merely what he desires. But the special feature of modern society is the revival of the old idea of the supremacy of the State.

Everyone is agreed that the State, as the guardian of the public weal, has the duty of controlling distribution, and of intervening, when distribution fails to take place spontaneously in accordance with justice and the public interest, in order to bring about what is called a re-distribution of income.

Attempts are made, for example, to carry out this re-distribution for the benefit of the family, and in many recent constitutions and declarations of the rights of man the principle is laid down that a married man and a parent are entitled to an income sufficient to provide for the family and bring up the children. In former days the family was left to its own devices, and parents of modest means found themselves dependent on public charity.

In the same way, the principle of social insurance lays upon the State the obligation of watching over the security of the workers; and these principles, though still imperfectly applied, are nevertheless no longer disputed. Accordingly the State allocates from the national revenue a sum sufficient to enable every parent to bring up his children, and to guarantee security to every worker. The principle of re-distribution commands universal assent; it is only over methods that differences of opinion arise.

This re-distribution is carried out partly by taxation. Higher and higher taxes are imposed on large fortunes, the income tax on which amounts to ninety or ninety-five per cent. in the socially most advanced countries. Death duties are levied at a similar rate. The ancients maintained that the rich owed the whole of their superfluous wealth to the poor; but the ancient State had no means of compelling them to carry out their duty. The modern State disposes of far greater means of compulsion. Accordingly it lays down appropriate subsistence levels for each social class. A man with an income of £20,000 will be left with £2,000 on which to live respectably, if not on a princely scale: the State re-distributes the remainder. A man with an income of £100,000 will be left with £5,000.

By this means extremes of both wealth and poverty are abolished. The modern State has the power to do this because it possesses the requisite technical apparatus, and because it can provide public services beyond the means of the rulers of former times. It must be added that those who are deprived of the greater part of their income usually feel extremely aggrieved, offer all the resistance they can, and invoke various principles in justification of their interests. In this connection it is interesting to note that the modern State is merely carrying out, on its own scale, what Cajetan considered to be the duty of the judge, and what St Thomas considered to be the function of the ruler.

Here we are moving on a different plane from that of charity, which is chiefly if not exclusively a matter of individual and personal assistance to the poor. Nowadays the question is rather one of cooperation for the public good, an idea approximating to what the ancients called the virtue of munificence, which they also regarded as a duty incumbent on the rich.

It is easy to see how times have changed. In former days the sole means of inducing the rich to fulfil their duty was by exhortation, to which the majority lent a deaf ear. Today the State, as the representative of the public weal, fixes a portion of the revenue which will meet the vital requirements of each social class, and re-distributes the remainder by taxation in accordance with the demands of the social order. The novelty of this procedure resides solely in the ability of the modern State to carry it out. The principle is indisputable, and is indeed no longer disputed. Controversy turns only on problems of application and, as often as not, of expediency.

Another kind of re-distribution is exemplified by what the American sociologist and economist Lewis Mumford calls "basic communism", which he contrasts with Marxist communism. Basic communism takes for its point of departure the proposition that "everyone, like the child in a family, is a member of a community", and that the social heritage of the community is shared by each one of its members. Consequently each member, merely by belonging to the community, has a right to the benefits which it confers. As examples of this basic communism, Mumford points to water-supply and compulsory free education; to which he might have added road maintenance, street lighting, sewage disposal and the public health service.

Moreover this basic communism can express itself in various ways. The State, besides supplying certain services free, can so re-distribute the available resources as to enable every citizen to afford the services which must be paid for. Whether education is free, or whether parents are supplied with the means to pay for it, the result is the same: it is all a question of expediency. Similarly the State can assume part responsibility for certain charges, as where it subsidizes baking or mining in order to keep down the price of bread or coal, or provides cheap transport for certain categories of workers and schoolchildren, thus enabling the poorer classes to live outside the great cities: again it is a question of expediency.

In any case, whatever the method employed, it is the function of the State to distribute the national income in such a way as to supply every member of the community with the amenities which modern civilization brings within the reach of all.

PAPAL PRONOUNCEMENTS

The outline given above does not meet with universal recognition. At the present moment the views of the pure economists are quite clear, as is proved by a perusal of Samuelson's *Economics*, a text-book in American secondary schools which we mention because the United States are considered to be the stronghold of capitalism and *laissez-faire*.

Economic problems, however, are confused by politico-social-religious controversies, by the opposition between neo-liberalism, or the economy of the free market, and dogmatic communism, by the passionate debates engendered by conflicting interests, and by religious interference, communism in particular being violently anti-religious and materialistic. The result is that most people are perplexed and alarmed when confronted with an unambiguous doctrine derived from Christian tradition.

In the present state of affairs Catholics are fortunate in having for their guide the teachings of the Holy See. As we have already observed, the principle according to which natural resources are, by intention, common property, has been increasingly emphasized by the papacy during the course of the twentieth century. All we need do here is quote, without comment, some pronouncements of recent popes, which for our purposes speak for themselves. It is our duty to give them a respectful hearing and allow them to govern our conduct. After what has been said, it will be recognized how closely they follow tradition, and how well they meet the needs and aspirations of the modern world.

Furthermore, we shall content ourselves with quoting only a few typical passages, referring the reader for further information to specialized studies of the subject.

Our first two quotations are from the encyclical of Pius XI, *Quadragesimo Anno* (1931):

> For then only will the economic and social order be soundly established and attain its ends, when it offers to all and each all those goods which the wealth and resources of nature, technique, and the social organization of economic affairs can give. These goods should be sufficient both to supply all necessities and reasonable comforts, and to uplift men to that higher standard of life which, provided it be used with prudence, is not only of no hindrance, but is of singular help, to virtue.... Wealth therefore, which is constantly being augmented by social and economic progress, must be so distributed amongst the various individuals and classes of society, that the needs of all ... be thereby satisfied ... and the distribution of created goods must be brought into conformity with the demands of the common good or social justice.[1]

Our next quotation is from the encyclical *Divini Redemptoris* (1937) on atheistic communism:

> To achieve this end demanded by the pressing needs of the common welfare, the wealthy classes must be induced to

[1] *Selected Papal Encyclicals and Letters*, 1896–1931, London, Catholic Truth Society, 1939.

assume those burdens without which human society cannot be saved nor they themselves remain secure. However, measures taken by the State with this end in view ought to be of such a nature that they will really affect those who actually possess more than their share of capital resources, and who continue to accumulate them to the grievous detriment of others.[2]

It is interesting to note that this passage occurs in the encyclical directed against communism, whereas big capitalists are in the habit of bringing charges of communism or crypto-communism against anyone advocating measures in accordance with the papal teaching.

We now come to Pius XII. We select for quotation one single but lengthy passage which provides one of the finest and most comprehensive surveys of our subject. It occurs in the radio message of 1st June, 1941, on the occasion of the fiftieth anniversary of the encyclical *Rerum Novarum*. Every word deserves to be read with the closest attention.

All men, considered as living creatures endowed with reason, derive from nature the fundamental right to make use of the material goods of the earth, though the detailed regulation of the exercise of this right may be left to the human will and to the legal system of the State. An individual right of this kind is not to be abrogated in any way, not even by other unquestionable and recognized rights to goods.

No doubt the natural order, since it proceeds from God, calls also for private property and the free traffic in goods by exchange and gift, as also for the control by the authority of the State of both these institutions. Nevertheless all these things remain subordinate to the natural purpose of material goods, and are not to be dealt with apart from the first and fundamental right by which the use of goods is granted to all men; rather must they serve to make possible the exer-

[2] *The Papal Encyclicals in their Historical Context*, edited by Anne Fremantle, New York, New American Library of World Literature, 1956.

cise of that right in accordance with the end in view. Only
in this way is it both possible and lawful to secure that the
use of material goods imparts to society the blessings of
peaceful productivity and healthy stability, instead of giving
rise to a state of instability breeding strife and jealousy, and
given over to the pitiless interplay of strength and weakness. . . .

The essential rôle of every public authority ought to consist in safeguarding the sacred rights of the individual to the
end that he may fulfil his duties. This is the true meaning
of that *common good* which the State is called upon to
promote.

Likewise the national economy, itself the result of the
labours of men working together in the community which
constitutes the State, has no other end than to secure unceasingly those material conditions which will permit the
full development of the life of the individual citizen. When
this object is attained and maintained a country may
properly be called rich, because its welfare, and consequently
the individual right of all its citizens to the use of material
goods will have been achieved in conformity with the
Creator's plan.

These considerations help us to understand that a
country's economic wealth consists not in an abundance of
goods calculated purely and simply according to their value,
but in the fact that this abundance of goods represents and
provides a real and effective material foundation for the
proper material progress of its members.[3]

The popes have no need to study modern economics.
They are applying to our own times the traditional teaching
of the Church, imbued with that spirit of brotherly love
which ought to prevail among men. It only remains for
Christians to follow the lead of the papacy in order to be
efficient promoters of the common good, which is the good
of all, of order, peace and social welfare.

[3] Wynne, John, *The Great Encyclical Letters of Leo XIII*, New
York, Benziger, 1903.

CHAPTER VII

THE RIGHT OF
OWNERSHIP

In the ancient world the disposal and management of goods were based on ownership, which in consequence became the corner-stone of the economic system. Now today we are confronted with a phenomenon which is at first sight disconcerting: economists, as we have seen, no longer concern themselves with the right of ownership. The Church, on the other hand, bears it constantly in mind. Our quotations have shown that the popes, nearly every time that they deal with economic questions, refer to the right of ownership. Actually, Catholics are almost the only people to mention the subject.

The indifference of the economists is explained by the fact that economics is a scientific method of studying production and distribution with a view to securing the welfare of the community. The Church concerns herself with the right of ownership because she discerns in it a moral value. Economists are not interested in moral considerations: the Church is not interested in economics, except in so far as it has moral effects. The Church enters the economic field only to assert the principles of morality. To the Church, ownership seems an important element in social morality:

she therefore pays particular attention to ownership as constituting a moral, that is a human, value.

Moreover, ownership is nowadays undoubtedly the most original item in Christian social philosophy. We must first inquire into the reasons for this, and then consider the way in which this concern for ownership leads to a conception of ownership which enables Christian social philosophy to pursue an independent course between liberal or capitalist ideologies on the one hand, and socialism on the other.

THE CHRISTIAN JUSTIFICATION OF THE RIGHT OF OWNERSHIP

The Church is concerned with man and with man's values. In what does the benefit of ownership to man consist?

One of the points on which Pius XII dwells most insistently in his messages and speeches is that private ownership constitutes an essential guarantee of the dignity of man.

> The Church aspires to bring it about that private ownership should become, in accordance with the plans of the divine wisdom and with the laws of nature, an element in the social system, a necessary incentive to human enterprise, and a stimulus to labour; all this for the benefit of the temporal and spiritual ends of life, and consequently for the benefit of the freedom and dignity of man created in the image of God, who in the beginning granted to man for his service dominion over created things (*Radio message*, September 1st, 1944).

The dignity of man: no man is really free unless he owns enough property to make him master of his own fate. All history shows that the man without property is at the mercy of whoever will provide him with a living. The abolition of slavery puts an end to human exploitation only to the extent in which it provides a man with property, thus enabling him to win his independence. The labour unrest of the nineteenth century was caused by the beneficiaries of legal freedom being prevented from making use of their freedom. A propertyless proletariat can be worse off than a slave. It can pay an employer to give better treatment to a slave than to an employee who is legally free but is in practice at the mercy of his boss on whom he depends for his wages.

Ownership therefore ensures that a man may be free to develop himself. "It is on man that the altogether personal obligation falls of maintaining and bringing to greater perfection his own material and spiritual life" (Pius XII, *Radio message*, June 1st, 1941).

There is an obvious connection between this teaching and the Christian view of personality. Human personality is the highest value we know on earth. The State and all other institutions are designed to minister to it. All social organization is directed to providing man with the means of self-development, in which ownership has a leading part to play.

Ownership is equally important for the family. The Church has never ceased to champion the right of a man to found a family, and of parents to have the last word in the education of their children. There is a right to be claimed from those in authority, and a duty to be observed between husband and wife, and between parents and the children for whom they are responsible.

"Only private ownership can provide the head of a family with the healthy freedom he requires to carry out the duties allotted to him by the Creator for the physical, spiritual and religious well-being of his family" (Pius XII, *Radio message*, June 1st, 1941).

"Nature dictates that a man's children, who carry on, so to speak, and continue his own personality, should be by him provided with all that is needful to enable them to keep themselves honourably from want and misery amid the uncertainties of this mortal life" (Leo XIII, *Rerum Novarum*, 1891).[1]

Ownership is essentially connected with labour. It is "in a quite special manner the natural fruit of labour, the result of strenuous activity on the part of the man who acquires it thanks to his active desire to secure and improve by his efforts a living for himself and his family, and to create for himself and his family a field of freedom, not only in economic but in political, cultural and religious matters" (Pius XII, *Radio message*, September 1st, 1944).

The three terms—labour, freedom, family—are thus seen to be interconnected. Man has a sovereign right over his own person: his only superior is God. Man's industry is his form of self-expression: hence his rightful claim to the products of his industry. Among these products ownership occupies a foremost place by guaranteeing his own and his family's independence.

The importance attached by the Church to ownership is readily explained. It is not a question of national income and its distribution; it is a question of man and his dignity, of his being allowed to live his own life, to found a family and bring up his children.

But what of poverty? How is this attitude to be reconciled with the injunction, itself an essential element of the Christian religion, to despise material goods?

We have seen that Christian poverty is not incompatible with a man's using material goods to fulfil his human vocation, and we have also seen that poverty, as it is practised in institutions such as the religious orders, involves a

[1] Wynne, John, *The Great Encyclical Letters of Leo XIII*, New York, Benziger, 1903.

renunciation of family life and the social activities of this world. Now in speaking of poverty we are referring neither to a social problem nor to an individual ideal. What we have to ask ourselves is whether, at the social level, man is entitled to freedom at the hands of his fellow men, whether considered as individuals or as represented by the State. Man is master of his fate and of his vocation. Christianity has given a higher place than any other religion to the dignity of man and to his lordship over the earth. From the social point of view, the first requisite is to make man secure in his independence. It is at this point that ownership has its part to play. Thereafter it rests with the individual to decide his own fate.

OWNERSHIP IN THE SERVICE OF MAN

After all that has been said, it is scarcely necessary to add that the Church favours the extension of the right of ownership.

Ownership is at the same time an incentive to labour and its reward. In the same way as a man performs his duty to society by working, so there is a sense in which it is work that constitutes the dignity of man. Similarly, it ought to be possible for every man to become a property owner, so that he may continue to enjoy the dignity which is both expressed and guaranteed by his labour. When the popes speak of the origin of property, it is to labour that they constantly revert.

The dignity of man shows itself in work, and it is essentially work that entitles a man to ownership. It is the duty of a healthy social system to bring ownership within the reach of every worker.

It was the condition of the working classes which caused the Church to concern herself with the social problem. The first of the great social encyclicals, *Rerum Novarum*, was entitled "On the Condition of the Working Classes". Consequently we need not be surprised when the popes, in speaking of ownership, constantly refer to working class ownership. Now in nineteenth- and twentieth-century Europe it was the working man who was conspicuous by owning no property. It became a question of "granting every class of the community a modicum of private property" (Pius XII, *Radio message*, December 24th, 1942).

On the other hand ownership, although essentially connected with human industry and arising spontaneously from it, is justified by reasons transcending labour. It furnishes the means whereby a man may live a truly human life as his own master, freely pursuing his own ends and bringing up his family. This is a totally different attitude from that of liberalism, which asserts an abstract right of ownership regarded as an absolute and independent value which, once established, is interpreted as an absolute and unlimited right of the owner, who is released from any obligation corresponding to the advantages he enjoys. The liberal conception of property leads to the defence of existing properties only, that is of their proprietors. In practice this theory of ownership leaves the owners sacrosanct, while neglecting to take any step to diffuse the enjoyment of the right of ownership. Christianity considers ownership in its human aspect, as a safeguard of human dignity, and it is the duty of Christians to influence society in the direction of making the benefits of property available to all.

It follows that the Christian theory of ownership is contrary to both liberalism, which ends in capitalism, and to marxism which preaches the abolition of private property. Christianity opposes to liberalism its profound feeling for human equality and fraternity, and for the equal right of all men to develop themselves to the full in the maximum degree of independence. To marxism it opposes its concern for human independence and its profound and fundamental conviction that man is master of his fate, and that one of the chief objects of any social system is to guarantee this independence and provide every citizen with the means of enjoying it. We have said enough to demonstrate that the Christian theory of ownership is possibly the most original element in the teaching of the Church.

At the same time the Church, while insisting on the human value of ownership, attaches importance to property only to the extent in which it benefits man. Now there are forms of property which are not conducive to human progress.

Ownership is connected with labour, and throughout history there have been rich classes for whom ownership has been an excuse for idleness. No papal pronouncement has ever expressed approval of this kind of ownership.

When the popes mention the benefits deriving from ownership they generally have in mind more particularly the working man's possession of a house, which provides him with independence and a home for his family.

Property of this kind is a means to a better life. It is not an instrument of exploitation, a superfluity used for tyrannizing over one's fellow men.

Ownership is at the service of man. "Our aim should be not to abolish private property, which is the basis of the stability of family life, but to promote its diffusion as the reward for the industry of every working man and woman" (Pius XII, *Speech to Italian Workers*, June 13th, 1943).

The diffusion of property ought not to be left to chance. It is the province of the State to set up the requisite institutions. "What you both can and ought to aim at is a more just distribution of wealth, which is and remains an item in the programme of Catholic social theory" (Pius XII, *Speech to members of Catholic Action*, September 7th, 1947).

It follows that institutions have an important part to play.

"Ownership, like other elements of social life, is not absolutely rigid" (Pius XI, *Quadragesimo Anno*, 1931). And the pope recalls the teaching of Leo XIII in *Rerum Novarum* that "the defining of private possession has been left by God to man's own industry and to the laws of individual peoples". It is unnecessary to quote further, since the question has been dealt with by every pope from Leo XIII to Pius XII.

"Actually we see a frequent clash between the ever growing army of workers and those excessive accumulations of wealth which, under the cover of anonymity, have ended by abandoning their social function and making it well-nigh impossible for the working man to acquire any effective property of his own" (Pius XII, *Radio message*, September 1st, 1944).

Nevertheless the Church, while concerning herself chiefly with small property owners, declines to condemn any kind of ownership taken in itself. The reaction against liberalism has taken the form, in socialism, of a number of collectivist theories which tend to reduce the part played by private property, or even to abolish it altogether. In our own day there is a fairly strong movement which aims at abolishing the private ownership of the means of production.

Yet the right to ownership presupposes the right to save, whereby a man ensures his security by accumulating and putting by a permanent reserve of goods. Such savings can be made available to any one who is prepared to make some venture for the common good. Direct State control of public enterprise is not calculated to encourage that individual initiative which is the most important factor in the common welfare.

"Of its very nature the true aim of all social activity should be to help members of the social body, but never to destroy or absorb them" (Pius XI, *Quadragesimo Anno*).

We need dwell no further on these questions, which will be treated in greater detail in other volumes of this series. Our interest in ownership derives solely from the fact that the attitude of the Church towards this problem is one of the expressions of the Christian attitude towards money and the goods which it procures.

The use of material goods as a means of promoting man's spiritual growth carries with it the idea of ownership in the service of man. Ownership is healthy when it serves man, unhealthy when it corrupts him. The economic system cannot be divorced from the human purposes it subserves.

THE OBLIGATIONS OF OWNERSHIP

The primary function of private property is "in order that individuals may be able to provide for their own needs and those of their families" (Pius XI, *Quadragesimo Anno*). But at the same time the pope adds that "a man's surplus income is not left entirely to his own discretion".

In the ancient world the poor greatly outnumbered the rich. We have remarked on the untiring persistence with which the teachers of the Church continued to remind the rich of their duties. When Leo XIII published the encyclical *Rerum Novarum* the situation was substantially the same, as it still remains in many countries: unceasingly the popes have reminded the rich of their duties. We need say no more on this subject of the obligations of ownership, except to point out that it provides yet another example of the originality of Christian philosophy, which is filled with the spirit of brotherly love. The wealthy Christian does not rejoice in his wealth, which he knows imposes obligations on him. He loves not wealth but his fellow men, and looks on his wealth as a means of helping them.

Neither does a poor Christian covet wealth. But goods are common by intention, and however they may be distributed are intended to be used by all.

The obligations of ownership are an integral part of Christian philosophy. Liberalism, as we have seen, concerned itself solely with the right of ownership *per se*, without troubling to widen the exercise of the right. All its efforts are directed to preventing any restriction of the owner's right. Socialism is concerned with cutting down the amount of property in private ownership, even to the extent of abolishing private property altogether. Only Christianity, while defending private property, seeks to extend both its benefits and the obligations of its owners.

In the world today, the countries which lead the way in civilized welfare are also those in which property and prosperity are widely diffused. In these circumstances the obligations of ownership apear in a new light.

Side by side with the wealthy classes, whose obligations we have sufficiently explained, there has grown up a "middle class" which, if not rich, is at any rate comfortably off. We have seen how in the modern Welfare State covetousness gives rise to poverty in the midst of plenty. The problem of the obligations of ownership throws a new light on the Christian attitude towards money.

To be "comfortably off" is to possess an income larger than the minimum required to support life. It means that one has enough money to contemplate buying a radio or television set, a motor cycle, a car or labour-saving devices for the home, or to afford a holiday. An adequate income can be spent in a variety of ways, and calls for the exercise of what the ancients termed the duty of munificence.

The ancients, when they talked of munificence, had in mind a small number of extremely rich men. Today, however, the problem concerns also that increasing multitude of people who, although not rich, are comfortably off, and can combine together to practise the virtue of munificence by contributing, for instance, to the many varieties of clubs and societies.

Whenever there is a disaster, such as a flood or a serious accident involving great loss of life, subscriptions are opened, and the greater part of the sums collected are found to come from people of small means, who are generally also responsible for contributing the mountains of clothing, bed-clothes, furniture and every kind of household equipment. Refugee children do not usually find a home in a millionaire's mansion: it is the people of modest but comfortable means who practise these virtues of munificence, which they are now in a position to afford.

All these activities presuppose a widespread minimum standard of affluence. They could not possibly be carried out by an under-nourished class of slum-dwellers. It is fortunately true that there are rich people who have the decency to devote their wealth to the practice of the classical virtue of munificence, but they tend to be outnumbered by the growing class of the comfortably off who are ready to pool their modest resources for the good of society.

A fine example is provided by the Catholic Church in the United States, built and maintained entirely by the faithful. Now the American Catholics started from poverty, and even today few of them have become rich. The thousands and millions of contributions which provide for the upkeep of the Church are subscribed by Americans of modest means.

As I write these lines, Belgium has suffered the worst mining disaster of the present century. More than two hundred miners were trapped in the pit. A wave of pity swept the whole country, and funds were opened for the relief of the families of the victims. Within a few days the Christian unions collected five million Belgian francs and thirty-five million French francs, all contributed by people of small means anxious to show their sympathy with misfortune.

Such a state of affairs can exist only where a large working class has a certain amount of money to spare: it could not exist in an under-developed country where the mass of the population is living on the verge of starvation. No people can be induced to carry its share of the burden of public expenditure in all its forms unless the general standard of living is sufficiently high and wealth is widely distributed. Nor is it difficult to see how favourable are such conditions for the progress of mankind.

The asylum given in many countries to foreign refugee children is a notable demonstration of the growth of moral sentiment, which could not find expression if the bulk of the population were living below the poverty line.

In the matter of the diffusion of small ownership the encyclicals generally refer to the ownership of a house and plot of land; but this particular instance is only one example whose importance varies in different communities. In general, the idea is that every working class family should enjoy a competency slightly above the bare minimum, so that it should sometimes be able to take on a new responsibility or afford an exceptional expenditure, and should in any case be released from the daily anxiety of "making both ends meet".

Comparing this situation with the previously mentioned state of "want in the midst of plenty", we perceive the true nature of the spirit of Christianity, and how it imparts to man's employment of good that note of spiritual brotherliness which is the essence of the Christian view of ownership.

THE MYSTIQUE OF POVERTY IN THE TWENTIETH CENTURY

Confronted with the social security of the Welfare State many Christians are reacting by a vigorous assertion of the spiritual value of charity. The Church today is witnessing a religious revival on the pattern of the movement begun by St Francis of Assisi in the thirteenth century.

But St Francis lived in a world which was officially Christian. His reforms were confined to the conduct of the Church and of the religious orders, and were directed against the corruption to which the clergy, and the monasteries in particular, were exposed by their wealth. Today we find ourselves in a world no longer officially Christian, a world in which Christians, whose numbers vary from country to country, are bound to testify by their example to the Gospel of Christ. In order to live a life wholly devoted to God, a Christian seeks to maintain that the value of life depends on the extent to which it bears witness to Christ and to his charity; and for the accomplishment of this aim he feels he must free himself from the stranglehold of the pursuit of material well-being.

The movement may be seen at work in many directions. In the first place we find a multiplicity of new religious foundations, of which the most remarkable at the present moment are the Little Brothers and Little Sisters of Jesus, better know as the Little Brothers and Sisters of Charles de Foucauld, the name "little brothers" being inspired by that of the Friars Minor, the name given to his followers by St Francis. Their aim is to live a life of poverty among the most depressed classes of workers, and to share in their poverty and work. It is sometimes said that St Francis, if he returned to earth, would choose to become a working man, for in the modern world it is the workers who are preeminently "the poor".

Nor do they wish to own property, because they are aware that men become the slaves of property. They wish to be free to follow the call of God, and to earn their own living.

The same spirit of opposition to the Welfare State is displayed in the Christian centres which are springing up everywhere. We have already referred to these in our discussion of the standard of living: here we must emphasize the aspect of surrender to the will of God, which takes the form of a reaction against excessive security and attachment to material things. Thus we find families who, in spite of the widespread mania for ownership, are unwilling to become property owners, and a craving for the simple life which shows itself in different forms. Nowadays the refusal to accept all the conditions of the Welfare State is a sign of sharp reaction against the contemporary world.

We can now distinguish the two aspects of Christian philosophy. On the one hand there is the social attitude expressed in the social teaching of the Church, which aims at building a society which offers free scope for the development of all its members. On the other hand there are the pioneers of a Christianity in reaction against the characteristic evils of the modern world. The two are not contradictory, but the expression of two different points of view, the first taking the communal view of the structure of society, the second consisting in a reaction against the disorder of the modern world and taking its stand on the law of Christ against the materialism in which spiritual values and charity are swamped and lost.

CONCLUSION

Setting out from the Gospel we have analysed the attitude of Christ towards the rich and the poor. It is an attitude transcending that which shrinks from acknowledging the physical basis of human values and thus results in fostering a spiritual development denying the claims of that natural life of which God himself was the author, and which Christ took upon himself in the Incarnation to make it the means of entry into the Kingdom. We have seen the inestimable value placed by our Saviour on human personality, how it is the man who is to be redeemed, perfected and made a sharer in the supernatural life, and how it is in submission to God and in his service that the greatness of man consists.

We then traced the development of Christian thought through the centuries, with regard to the Christian attitude to money in particular, and more generally to material goods; and we noted the Christian attempt to use material goods in the service of the Kingdom instead of for the gratification of covetousness and pride.

Christ took account of all the circumstances of human life, with all the manifold demands which it makes on mankind. This all-embracing sympathy has always proved disconcerting. In his life on earth Christ was accused both of worldliness and of unworldliness. He loved the poor, and did not refuse the hospitality of the rich. Throughout the centuries the Church has adopted the same attitude and has encountered the same criticism.

Christian philosophy, always faithful to its love of poverty and its right use of riches, culminates in the twentieth century in the social teaching of the Church, whose

ideal of welfare consists in the brotherly distribution of
goods and in the subordination of property to the service
of man.

Everything on earth is at the service of man, and man
is at the service of God. To put it more accurately, it is
man's duty to serve the Kingdom of God on earth, for
which purpose he must first identify himself with the
Kingdom.

All material goods are at the service of man, and the
greatness of man consists in his spiritual value, in that
mental aptitude for recognizing God and enlisting in God's
service. The danger of material goods lies in man's tendency
to become immersed in them. A man cannot be the slave
of two masters, God and Mammon. Mammon is money.
Money is a slave, and ought not to be turned into a master.

Christianity is the only religion in the world which aims
at using material goods without being mastered by them,
with the object of developing the mind of man and guiding
him along the path of his spiritual destiny which ends in
God. No wonder that the modern popes are never weary
of repeating that, outside Christ and the way of salvation
which he has shown to us, there can be no fully balanced
development of man, no growth of that spiritual life which
has its beginning and end in God.

The ideal is the worldwide community of the brotherhood of man. In order to achieve it, one must avoid the
temptations offered by material goods and principally by
money. Money brings not only material enjoyment, but
power and a feeling of superiority over our fellow men
which prevents us from regarding them as brothers. Furthermore, such gifts as a man possesses should be used
not for selfish purposes, but for spreading the spirit of
fraternity throughout the community.

This is the goal towards which all roads lead, this is the

Kingdom of God. A worker for the Kingdom must strenuously cultivate that "poorness in spirit" without which there can be no virtue in either wealth or poverty. It is impossible to see God in the world or to attend to his voice and obey his will if the mind is centred on itself. A man's mind is centred on material goods only if he is centred on himself; but material goods are also centred on the Self.

In short, the features of the Saviour are discernible in every Christian who is truly "poor in spirit". The whole meaning of Christian life is that Christ lives in us. It is the duty of a Christian, by allowing Christ to indwell him, to bestow upon the world the gift of Christ's teaching and example. The behaviour of a Christian should be the behaviour of Christ, the presence of Christians in the world should be the abiding presence of Christ, wherever there are Christians Christ should be actively present, and the Kingdom which is "amongst us" should come into being whenever there are Christians to be found among men.

Today, more than ever, it is imperative for a Christian to learn to detach himself from the worship of material things for their own sake. The tendency of all modern civilization is not only, as perhaps in all previous ages, to immerse us in material things but to enslave us to the cult of material values. The tendency of the age, whether by publicity or the picture papers or the various forms of mass propaganda, is to instil the idea that happiness consists in material pleasures. It is the duty of Christians to combat this idea by constantly remembering not only that man's greatness is spiritual, but that this spiritual greatness derives from the fact that it is only in spirit that we approach God; in short, that the greatness of man is in God, and that it is in Christ and by Christ and the growth of his life in us that we approach God.

The goal of man's life on earth is to serve God and to draw near him. For its accomplishment there is required that spirit of detachment which is primarily the spirit of poverty, which alone enables us to use the material goods given us by God in accordance with his will. By this means we may achieve the purity which leads to God, and may become the forerunners of the community of brothers to which we are called by Christ.

"Make it your first care to find the Kingdom of God, and all these things shall be yours without the asking." The search is what matters: the rest will be added. The Christian attitude of detachment towards material things is designed solely to set us free to find the Kingdom.

SELECT BIBLIOGRAPHY

BRUEHL, Charles D.: *The Pope's Plan for Social Reconstruction*, New York, Devin Adair, 1954.

CRONIN, John S.: *Catholic Social Principles*, Milwaukee, Bruce, 1955.

GILL, Eric: *Christianity and the Machine Age*, London, Sheldon Press, 1940.

FREMANTLE, Anne (Ed.): *The Papal Encyclicals in their Historical Context*, New York, New American Library of World Literature, 1956.

HOLLIS, Christopher: *The Breakdown of Money*, London and New York, Sheed and Ward, 1937.

HUGHES, Philip: *The Popes' New Order: A Systematic Study of the Social Encyclicals and Addresses from Leo XIII to Pius XII*, London, Burns Oates, 1943.

REGAMEY, P. R., O.P.: *Poverty*, London and New York, Sheed and Ward, 1949.

Selected Papal Encyclicals and Letters, Vol. I, 1896–1931, London, Catholic Truth Society, 1939.

SOMERVILLE, H.: *Studies on the Catholic Social Movement*, London, Burns Oates, 1933.

WILLIAMS, M. J.: *Catholic Social Thought*, New York, Ronald Press, 1954.

WYNNE, John: *The Great Encyclical Letters of Leo XIII*, New York, Benziger, 1903.